Invitation to Person Centred Psychology

Tony Merry

W

Whurr Publishers Ltd
London

First published 1995 by
Whurr Publishers Ltd
19b Compton Terrace, London N1 2UN, England

Reprinted 1996 (twice)

British Library Cataloguing in Publication Data
A catalogue record for this book is available from the
British Library.

ISBN 1-897635-45-1

Photoset by Stephen Cary
Printed and bound in the UK by Athenaeum Press Ltd,
Gateshead, Tyne & Wear

Contents

Acknowledgements

Thanks are due to many people who helped with this book, including Windy Dryden, the Series Editor, for his help and encouragement.

Special thanks to Ms G. for giving her permission to use the transcript of her interview with Carl Rogers, and also to Valerie Henderson for permission from the USA.

Thanks to Geoffrey Court, Jeannette Weaver and Stephen de Brett for their immensely valuable contributions to the chapters on education. Thanks in particular to Geoffrey Court for giving permission to use material first published by the Tower Hamlets Primary Teachers Support Group and a special edition of the *Christian Action Journal*.

Thanks also to Bob Lusty for his help in the planning of the book, and to Rowan Bayne, Colin Lago and Paul Marchant for patiently reading through early drafts and for their expert comments and suggestions.

Finally, my heartfelt thanks to Janet Reeves for her encouragement, patience, warmth and love.

To Jan

Preface

This book is written for anyone interested in people. It is based on the work of Carl Rogers (1902–1987), a psychotherapist, researcher and teacher from the humanistic approach to psychology. Its main concerns are with human growth, development and communication, and its spirit is optimistic for the future of humankind. I hope it will appeal to people with little or no knowledge of psychology as much as to those studying at 'A' level or for a degree, and to those simply interested to extend their knowledge about people.

Humanistic psychology became more widely known in the early 1960s with the formation of the American Association for Humanistic Psychology and the publication of the *Journal of Humanistic Psychology*. In Britain, the Association for Humanistic Psychology also publishes a journal – *Self and Society*. Humanistic psychology is an approach to psychology generally, rather than a specific school of thought. This book describes the contributions of the Person Centred Approach (PCA) to the development and refinement of humanistic psychology theory and practice.

The book is an *invitation* to person centred psychology, rather than a comprehensive description of it. Each chapter begins by posing the kind of question that is often asked about people, and then offers some ideas, perspectives and theory that might shed some light – always, of course, from a person centred point of view. Wherever possible, I have included 'real life' case studies and examples in an attempt to show how person centred psychology involves encounters with real people in everyday life. The case studies, with one exception (Jake in Chapter 3), are of real people used either with their permission, or drawn from previously published material.

Person centred psychology began life as an approach to counselling and psychotherapy. Much of what Carl Rogers and his colleagues learned about people came as a result of meeting and trying to understand them in therapy as they struggled with the problems of living.

Later, this learning was broadened to include people in groups and communities. The story of how Carl Rogers developed his theories and approach from working with individuals to working with groups and organisations is reflected in the pages of this book.

There are four sections. Section I introduces some theory and philosophy; Section II explores issues of individual feelings, behaviour and relationships; Section III is on education, teaching and learning and is the first of two sections that explore applications of person centred psychology with groups and organisations. The last section discusses person centred efforts to explore tensions and conflicts between hostile groups. Each section begins with a brief introduction in which I outline the main concerns and key issues.

I have used the term *person centred psychology* throughout the book to include the theory, philosophy and applications of Carl Rogers' work. The term *Person Centred Approach* (PCA) is also used, but in this book it refers to ways in which person centred psychology is applied to real life situations.

I had the good fortune of working with Carl Rogers three times towards the end of his life. I found him exactly as I expected him to be from reading his books – warm, good humoured, deeply interested in people, and the best listener I have ever met. I hope this book does his work justice.

Section I
Theory and Philosophy of the Person

Chapter 1
Introduction: The Origins and Growth of Person Centred Psychology

Person centred psychology developed from the work of Carl Rogers, an American psychologist and psychotherapist who died in 1987. It is one of the most influential of a group of approaches to the development and enhancement of human experience which, taken together, have become known as 'Humanistic Psychology'.[1] The purpose of this introductory chapter is to help you place person centred psychology in the context of psychology generally, and to raise some of the issues discussed in more detail later on.

Humanistic psychology is concerned with the quality of life — how people grow, develop and become who they are. It offers some ways of helping those in distress, and of making everyday life more fulfilling. Humanistic psychologists are concerned with issues like creativity, love, intrinsic nature, being, becoming, individuality, meaning, perception, reality, unity and self-consistency.

Carl Rogers, along with Abraham Maslow, Rollo May and others, was one of the early pioneers in this new approach to psychology. Rogers is best known for his work in counselling and psychotherapy, but his ideas became influential in many other areas, like education, community work and conflict exploration.

Like Rogers, Maslow became disillusioned with what he saw as the mainstream 'academic' psychology of his day, and he looked for ways of including more human values in psychology. Unlike Rogers though, Maslow was not a trained psychotherapist and did very little counselling or psychotherapy work. He was particularly interested in what he called 'self-actualised' people, that is, people who were able to

---

[1] The term 'humanistic' here should not be confused with 'humanism' which is a belief system putting human interests first, and rejects the supernatural or spiritual. Spirituality is an important theme in humanistic psychology, and more recently people with an interest in this aspect of human experience have begun to develop a new form of psychology called 'Transpersonal Psychology'.

operate in the world in a more complete way, using their capacities and creativity to the full. He described such people as having autonomy, spontaneity, and a high regard for aesthetic values. They also seemed more involved in causes or missions, displayed greater acceptance of themselves and others, and were more able to have mystical or transcendent experiences (e.g. Maslow, 1971).

Maslow and Rogers shared the idea that people have an inherent tendency to become fully functioning individuals able to express more and more of their potential. They also agreed that this tendency provides the underlying motivation for all human behaviour, though they did not agree entirely about the process of self-actualisation – the psychological means by which people become more fully functioning.

Rollo May represented the more European strands of thinking of existentialism and phenomenology (e.g. May, 1969). He had interests in art, creativity, mythology and the origins of evil, destructive behaviour – issues that are still very much alive in modern humanistic psychology.

Three Approaches to the Person – A Brief Comparison

To the humanistic psychologist, people are social beings searching for more enhancing, more meaningful ways of living, but this does not mean denying the destructive and anti-social side of human existence. This optimistic stance on the question of human nature contrasts with the more pessimistic view adopted by Freud and many of his followers, but Freud's emphasis on childhood development, and how early relationships profoundly affect us all our lives, finds many echoes within humanistic psychology.

Freud and Psychoanalysis

Freud's major contribution was his emphasis on unconscious aspects of personality. Often used is the iceberg analogy – what we are conscious of in ourselves is only a very small part of the story, the rest lies hidden underneath. Freud also described what he called a 'preconscious' where things reside of which we are not immediately aware, but are quite easily accessible with a little effort. The conscious mind contains those things that are in our immediate awareness.

Freud also provided a structural model of the mind consisting of the *id*, *ego* and *superego*. The *id* is the most primitive part of the personality, and is the original system with which we enter the world. The *id* makes no judgements about right and wrong, and has no inhibitions – it is where instincts or drives reside. According to Freud, there are two instincts, one of which (life instinct) is thought to have *psychic energy* (called *libido)*, the other (the death instinct) is thought to have destructive energy.

The *ego* is guided by the 'reality principle' and strives for objectivity – the ability to differentiate between what is desired and what is available. The ego is affected by the demands of others, and if the ego is allowed only limited outlets for instinctual energy, there will be a build - up of tension resulting in anxiety and inefficient functioning.

The *superego* contains the values and standards of parents and others incorporated into the individual's personality, and can be thought of as a system of internal judgements or even as a conscience. The superego can be very punishing and critical and lead to feelings of guilt, or it can lead to feelings of pride and heightened self-esteem.

Freud's view was that humankind has an inherent tendency towards destructive behaviour as a consequence of the death instinct. Although he believed that this destructive tendency could be controlled, or redirected, he maintained a fairly pessimistic attitude about the ability of human societies to live in peace.

The form of psychotherapy that Freud developed – psychoanalysis – involves a reliving of the past. As early feelings and emotional conflicts emerge, patients tend to associate them with the analyst, a process called *transference*. Patients come to view the analyst as different personalities, as an overcontrolling mother, or as a distant and cold father, for example. Working through these transferences enables patients to relive early relationships and bring them to a more emotionally satisfactory conclusion.

Skinner and Behaviourism

There are also major differences between humanistic psychology and another major branch of psychology – behaviourism. Behaviourism is associated with the eminent psychologist B.F. Skinner, but the founder of behaviourism was John B. Watson who took the view that psychology should be the study of behaviour rather than the mind. Skinner developed this original idea, and concentrated on the effects of the environment in determining behaviour. He believed that each of us inherits a unique genetic structure that predisposes us to find some environmental conditions satisfying (he used the term 'reinforcing') and others not. Of course, he knew that internal events (feelings and thoughts) existed, but he did not consider them to be the causes of behaviour. For Skinner, it was more important to focus attention on environmental factors because they can be directly observed and, if possible, changed, whereas internal conditions cannot be observed and altered directly.

The application of Skinner's ideas by psychotherapists is usually referred to as 'behaviour modification'. They attempt to discover the circumstances that produced problems in people's behaviour, and then to provide ways that modify that behaviour. A simple example is with a child who often has temper tantrums. A first step might be to ignore the tantrums, but to reinforce behaviour that is more desirable by giving rewards like attention and approval. Similarly, in homes for disturbed children, for example, there can be a system involving a 'token economy'. This is where children can collect tokens for performing some specified behaviour and then exchange them later for rewards like trips out or other privileges.

Rogers and the Person Centred Approach

Carl Rogers began to develop his approach to psychology during the early 1940s. Originally interested in counselling and psychotherapy, his early work was known as 'non-directive' psychotherapy. This was based on the hypothesis that therapists cannot decide the directions in which people should change and develop, but should help clients explore their needs from their own point of view, and discover their own internal resources. Later, Rogers and his colleagues started calling their work 'client centred therapy' to emphasise that it was clients who were at the centre of the process, not techniques and methods.

Rogers thought that the things he had learned about people in the therapy room could be transferred to other human problems, and the term 'Person Centred Approach (PCA)' began to be used. This indicates that change and development results from meetings (or encounters) between people as equals, and that the 'person' of the therapist also has a significant part to play. The term 'Person Centred Approach' is now the most commonly used when referring to Rogers' set of ideas about helping people change and discover more about who they are. In this book, the term 'person centred psychology' includes theoretical and philosophical concepts, as well as the practical ideas employed in applying theory and philosophy to real life events.

The central hypothesis of person centred psychology is that:

> Individuals have within themselves vast resources for self-understanding and for altering their self-concepts, basic attitudes, and self-directed behaviour; these resources can be tapped if a definable climate of facilitative psychological attitudes can be provided (Rogers, 1980: 115).

At the risk of over-simplification, the differences between Rogers, Skinner and Freud can be summed up quite quickly. Rogers thought that human beings are essentially social, creative and striving for full realisation (or 'actualisation') of their potentials, whereas Freud was concerned that human beings have a dark, destructive core that needs to be kept under control. Skinner was concerned far less with internal processes, and believed that a combination of genetic factors and environmental conditioning created certain kinds of behaviour at the expense of others.

Freud developed a sophisticated model of the functioning of the mind, and described a number of developmental stages that people go through on their journey towards psychological maturity. Rogers also developed a theory of personality but he presented it in much more general terms. His optimistic view of human nature led him to concentrate more on the processes of change and development as continuous throughout life. (An excellent and detailed comparison of Freud, Rogers and Skinner can be found in Nye, 1991.)

Humanistic Psychology and the Question of Power

Humanistic psychology in general, and person centred psychology in particular, is concerned with questions of power and its distribution. In the context of counselling and psychotherapy, for example, the conventional view holds that the therapist is an expert in sorting out emotional difficulties, and the patient is the consumer of this expertise. This is sometimes referred to as the 'medical model' and is a reflection of the wider social reality that exists within our patriarchal culture.

Traditionally, for example, men have been, and still are, more powerful than women in terms their economic power and their status and role power. Wherever power imbalances operate in the wider culture, between black and white, male and female, child and adult, gay and straight, they are likely to operate within all individual human relationships. The role of 'expert' and 'layperson' also reflects an unequal distribution of power where one is dependent on the other, and the danger in such situations is for people to feel overpowered by experts, rather than helped by them.

Humanistic psychology is not politics, but it does have a political dimension in that it challenges power structures where they appear to overpower the people who are governed by them. The person centred view of therapy, for example, is one where the therapeutic process is shared as equally as possible between therapist and client. The therapist's aim is to help clients recognise their inner capacities for change and growth. In this sense, the therapist is more like a companion on a journey than an expert guide.

An Actualising Tendency

At the very heart of humanistic psychology lies the assumption that there exists in all organic life a tendency towards more complex organisation, the fulfilment of potential, and the actualisation of the 'self' – the process of becoming all we are capable of becoming. Carl Rogers and Abraham Maslow both called this the 'actualising tendency'. The premise that there exists such a tendency, and that human beings are essentially trustworthy, forms a key part of the philosophy of all of humanistic psychology, not only in the world of therapy and counselling, but also in the applications of humanistic psychology ideas more generally.

An Existential View of Living

Running in parallel with this constructive view of human nature is a second philosophical strand also underpinning all of humanistic psychology – the philosophy of existentialism.

Existentialism includes the idea that people construct whatever meaning they can from their experiences, and that such meaning is likely to be significantly different for everybody. It suggests that we behave in ways that match our subjective awareness of ourselves and the environment in which we live. The implication is that even if 'objective reality' exists, it does not determine our behaviour, but the way we perceive and make sense of reality does.

Take, for example, two people watching the same film on television. They both see the same images and hear the same words, but to one the film is all about human relationships, love, overcoming difficulties and the triumph of the human spirit in adversity. To the other, the film is all about the futility of trying to change things for the better, the advisability of not getting involved in other people's business and the need to put oneself first.

These two people are experiencing the same thing, but are constructing different meanings from the experience. Each has a different set of values, and has a different life story, so the scenes in the film have different meanings for them. The events portrayed do not touch them in the same way, and their responses to what they see and hear are profoundly influenced by what has happened to them in the past and how they see themselves as persons in the present.

A term that goes hand in hand with existentialism is 'phenomenology', which can be thought of as a method or means of understanding 'reality'. It emphasises the importance of each person's immediate awareness or conscious experience in determining what is, for them, reality. Rogers, and other humanistic psychologists, maintain that it is knowing how these individual perceptions of reality are constructed that is the key to understanding human behaviour.

The Development of the 'Self'

Every major approach to human experience and development has put forward a theory to account for how personality is formed, and tries to explain people's behaviour from the point of view of this theory. In person centred psychology, the theory of personality is often referred to as a 'phenomenological theory', or 'self theory'. This theory provides a fairly broad picture of how people develop a concept of 'self' (that which enables you to differentiate yourself from the rest of humanity), and what the building blocks of that 'self' might be.

As children, we interact with our environment, including the people in it, and we learn certain things about life and about ourselves as a result. We learn, for example, what is acceptable and unacceptable behaviour by monitoring and evaluating the reactions of others. We have a need to gain love, support and protection from those around us, and a need to develop a sense of self-worth, or self-esteem. Because we are so dependent on parents or other care givers for our survival, however, we tend to be more sensitive to the reactions and evaluations of others than we are to our own feelings and wishes.

For Rogers, like many other theorists, early childhood influences the kind of person each one of us might become. However, unlike many approaches to personality, person centred theory believes that significant changes to personality are possible in later life. In Chapter 3, we look in detail at the way personality is thought to develop. An understanding of it is important if we are to understand why person centred psychology places such great emphasis on the qualities of the relationships we develop with other people.

The Importance of Relationships

Counselling and psychotherapy remains the major application of person centred theory, but this book explores other applications as well. In all cases, there is a strong emphasis on the qualities of the relationships that develop among the people concerned, whether, for example, they are between client and therapist, teacher and learner or parent and child.

Just about every form of psychotherapy emphasises the relationship between client and therapist (or counsellor). In person centred psychology, the nature of all relationships is important in influencing how we develop as individuals, and how we can contribute to the well-being of others.

In the psychodynamic tradition (based on the theories of Freud), psychotherapeutic relationships provide the means whereby old, perhaps child-like ways of relating become reproduced in the present. This is the phenomenon of *transference*; in other words patterns of behaviour that were learned by the young child, and feelings that may have become repressed, become exposed and can be talked through as part of the process. In the psychodynamic tradition, long-term therapy cannot proceed without transference, and psychodynamic therapy often brings transference feelings into the open in quite a direct way.

Freud and his followers believe that transference is not confined to the analyst's office, but that all relationships contain elements of it. We are always relating to people based on our experiences of past relationships, whether we are conscious of those experiences or not. Person centred psychology goes along with this to a certain extent, though transference is dealt with differently. In person centred psychology, it is acknowledged that our present day relationships are built on, or at least affected by, our learning from past encounters with people. The way we relate to others is also affected by our sense of self-esteem.

The 'Core Conditions' of Successful Relationships

For any form of therapy to proceed effectively, the therapist needs to be someone who can inspire confidence and trust, who is respectful and who can provide a safe environment within which clients feel able to talk about themselves. Therapists of all orientations believe in the fundamental importance of a good therapeutic relationship, but Rogers went further than perhaps anyone else by describing three characteristics of such relationships which, if present would enable therapy to take place and if absent would prevent it. These three characteristics are: that the therapist experiences and communicates a deep empathic understanding of the client's 'inner world'; that the therapist remain congruent, real or authentic in her relationships with clients; and that the therapist experiences and communicates unconditional positive regard for the client.

A clear implication of Rogers' work is that the variety of techniques available do not, in themselves, have any specific value other than how far they contribute to the presence (or absence) of these core conditions. It is thought that when empathy, congruence and unconditional positive regard are present in *any* relationship (not just in therapy), those relationships are more likely to be successful and creative.

Influences from the East

Many humanistic psychologists have been influenced by some of the Eastern philosophies such as Zen and Taoism. Briefly, Zen is a branch of Buddhist thought that says that 'the truth' resides in the heart and can be discovered by meditation and self-mastery.

Humanistic psychology includes efforts to help people contact their experience directly, with as little distortion as possible, and this has real parallels with some of the meditative practices of Zen. Buddhism is also very present oriented, focusing on here-and-now experiences, and this is another characteristic of many humanistic psychology practices.

Carl Rogers

Carl Rogers was born in Oak Park near Chicago, Illinois, the fourth child in a family of six. His father bought a farm when Carl Rogers was twelve years old, and it was here that Rogers' interest in science and nature was born and flourished. Originally, Rogers had thoughts of making a career in agriculture, but later began to entertain ideas about joining the Ministry, perhaps prompted by the devout religious lifestyle of his parents. It was not until at college in New York that he began to develop an interest in psychology – an interest that was to last the remainder of his life. His first professional role as a psychologist was with the Rochester Society for the Prevention of Cruelty to Children, at the Rochester Child Study Center, New York.

One of his most important contributions was to record and publish complete transcripts of psychotherapy interviews. In the early days this was a cumbersome task as interviews had to be recorded on disc, each disc lasting only a few minutes before needing to be changed, but somehow he and his team managed to collect many hours of live interviews. He was the first person ever to do this, and so was the first to open up the mysteries of the psychotherapeutic process and make his work and ideas more generally available.

It was largely as a result of these recordings that Carl Rogers and his colleagues were able to examine the therapeutic process in detail and begin the task of determining what factors seemed to help or hinder clients. This was the start of perhaps the most comprehensive research effort ever undertaken into determining the characteristics of effective psychotherapy. One of the outcomes of this research was the publication, in 1957, of a paper entitled 'The necessary and sufficient conditions of therapeutic personality change' (Rogers, 1957a).

This was the paper that outlined Rogers' formulation of what he considered to be the characteristics of an effective psychotherapeutic relationship. In it, Rogers described the three main attitudes or, 'ways of being', of therapists which, if present, would help clients to change in positive ways. The paper stimulated a great deal of comment and research and by 1984 C.H. Patterson was able to remark:

> There are few things in the field of psychology for which the evidence is so strong. The evidence for the necessity, if not the sufficiency, of the therapist conditions of accurate empathy, respect or warmth, and therapeutic genuineness is incontrovertible (Patterson, 1984).

Exactly what these 'necessary and sufficient' conditions mean in practice will be explored in detail in Chapter 10. Rogers' ideas were based on systematic research, and his claims were later substantiated in good measure by other independent researchers, although many are still critical of them.

Although Rogers was committed to the scientific process, he was a powerful advocate of new forms of research and new methods of inquiry that valued and were respectful of individual human experience. He wrote extensively about the need for a science of the person that could value the subjective, inner world as much as the more observable world of behaviour.

He developed and expanded the person centred theory of psychotherapy in ways that made it possible to make considerable contributions in the field of education, conflict exploration, and indeed any situation in which human communication is valued. He was a major inspiration behind the development of the intensive group experience that flourished in the 1960s (and still does today) known as the 'encounter group' or 'basic encounter group' (see Chapter 16). This broadening out of the theory became known as the Person Centred Approach (PCA).

He developed a concise and elegant personality theory, one of the most enduring and respected theories of personality to emerge from humanistic psychology, but it remained a puzzle to Rogers why it was not more widely read and incorporated into the teaching of psychology generally. This, however, has changed, and modern psychology textbooks that deal extensively with personality theory incorporate Rogers' work alongside that of Freud and others.

He also brought an appreciation and valuing of the positive, constructive and social side of human beings without ever denying their capacity for destructive behaviour. This side of Rogers' work has been much misunderstood, and this misunderstanding is often responsible for the charge that he was overly sentimental and naive in his approach to humankind.

Rogers put forward a new and, to some, quite revolutionary approach to working with people in distress, and many from the more traditional branches of psychology viewed him as something of a threat. Even from among those who saw themselves as being humanistic there were some who misunderstood and misrepresented his work. Person centred psychotherapy, for example, has been taught as if it were merely a set of techniques. This is a serious misrepresentation of Rogers who saw at the heart of successful psychotherapy an authentic meeting of equals in which clients were cared for and respected as people capable of positive change and growth for themselves.

For Rogers, the subjective world of experience was the most rewarding of all: 'Experience is, for me, the highest authority' (Rogers, 1961: 23). However, Rogers knew that experience and the way we make sense of it, needs to be checked and tested before we can rely on it with confidence: ' I enjoy the discovering of order in experience. It seems inevitable that I seek for the meaning or the orderliness or lawfulness in any large body of experience. It is this kind of curiosity, which I find it very satisfying to pursue, which has led me to each of the major formulations I have made' (Rogers, 1961: 24).

Perhaps more than anything else, Carl Rogers was a student of human communication. His life's work was dedicated to deepening his understanding of the processes by which people meet and endeavour to understand each other. He immersed himself in the lives of his clients trying always to listen to them and understand them. Above all, he prized this process of encountering and understanding others, and he saw communication as the key to personal and social change.

About this Book

This overview of the origins and development of person centred psychology specifically and humanistic psychology generally, though necessarily brief, provides the groundwork for a much more detailed review of theory, philosophy and application later on. This book poses the kinds of questions people often ask about human nature and 'what makes us tick', and explores how person centred psychology can provide some ways of thinking about them. Throughout the book I illustrate the ideas by including experiences of real people engaged in the struggle of trying to incorporate more humanistic values into their lives.

The book is divided into four sections. The first section tackles the basic philosophical and theoretical ideas that underpin person centred psychology. I offer some thoughts, arguments and evidence to show how person centred psychology sees personality development, what motivates us in life, and how the existence of evil and destructive behaviour can be explained whilst maintaining a positive and optimistic stance on questions of human nature.

The second section explores some questions about what it means to be human. We start with personal, internal processes like the development of a value system, and how we exercise (or are prevented from exercising) our free choice. We then move on to considering some aspects of human relationships in more detail, and, finally, we take a closer look at one quite unusual relationship – that between person centred therapist and client.

In Section III we move beyond the individual to the outside world – in this case to the world of school and education. I show how person centred psychology has a real contribution to make to the ways in which we educate our children. I look at how relationships between teachers and learners affect our experience of education, and how schools might be organised to provide a more person centred environment. In this section, I have drawn heavily on the experiences of people who work in schools and other educational organisations to show how they are overcoming the problems they face.

The final section moves out further into the world, and we tackle the most important issue of our times – how we can learn to live in peace with ourselves and those around us. We look at some of the influences that cultural and other differences have on helping relationships, and I discuss how person centred psychology can be applied in group settings. Carl Rogers' peace work and his concern with the exploration of conflict is, perhaps, the least well known aspect of his work. I finish this book with an exploration of how person centred psychology has tried to find new and perhaps more creative ways of approaching deep-seated conflicts among people.

Chapter 2
What Makes Us Tick?

This is a question about motivation, and is concerned with the extent to which human behaviour is either directed towards goals, however general, or is more random and all a matter of chance. It is also concerned with how far human behaviour is determined by genetic inheritance or environmental circumstances, or a combination of the two. The person centred point of view is that behaviour is a result of complex relationships between genetic make-up, environmental circumstances and individual choice, influenced by our innate tendency to seek fulfilment of potential.

Although I have put the question in very simple terms, it is a very complex one – what makes one person 'tick', for example the desire to be rich and famous, has no appeal for someone else. The way I have posed the question reflects one approach to thinking about people – that they are like machines, and some branches of psychology do take a view similar to this:

> I would conceive of man clearly in the robot end of the continuum. That is, his behaviour can be completely determined by outside stimuli. Even if man's behaviour is determined by internal mediating events such as awareness, or thinking, or anxiety or insight, these events can be manipulated by outside stimuli so that it is these stimuli which basically determine our behaviour (Krasner, 1965).

Actualisation

Carl Rogers, and other humanistic psychologists like Abraham Maslow, took a different view. They believed that human behaviour cannot be explained simply as resulting from the stimulation of external events. Rogers' theory includes the idea that people are born with an innate tendency to explore their environment, to learn from it and to seek more fulfilling and satisfying ways of living, a process Rogers called 'actualisation'. Actualisation is a built-in tendency or capacity of the person and happens whether you are aware of it or not. In Rogers' words:

> In my experience I have discovered man to have characteristics which seem inherent in his species, and the terms which at different times seemed to me descriptive of these characteristics are such terms as positive, forward-moving, constructive, realistic, trustworthy (Rogers, 1957b).

When biologists discuss animal behaviour, they talk about animals as having instincts, and they view these instincts as providing the motivation for animal behaviour. They include the instinct to reproduce, to seek nourishment and shelter for themselves and their young, to establish and defend territories and so on. The migratory journeys of some birds and fish are other examples of how instincts guide and determine animal behaviour. It is important to remember that instincts are not consciously controlled. The behaviour that results from them is not a matter of choosing from a number of possible alternatives. A bird does not decide whether to migrate or not, any more than fish to swim in shoals, or zebras to travel in herds. Though there are obvious similarities, I do not think it would be accurate to describe the actualising tendency simply as an instinct. An instinct usually refers to a fixed pattern of behaviour in response to a specific external stimulus. The actualising tendency is much more complex, and does not result in any specific or predictable behaviours.

In psychoanalytic terms people are thought to be born with certain instincts. Although I do not want to go too deeply into Freudian theory in a book about person centred psychology, it might help to understand Rogers better if we contrast his theories with those of Freud because the two are so different. This contrast will show how Rogers can be thought of as optimistic about human nature, while Freud took a far more pessimistic view.

Freud's Life and Death Instincts

Freud thought that people were born with both life instincts (Eros) and a death instinct. The life instincts guide the survival of the individual (and hence, the whole species), and Freud thought that the 'psychic energy' of instincts is responsible for human actions. The death instinct (the death wish), according to Freudian theory, originated in very early evolutionary history, but Freud thought that modern humankind still retains elements of this tendency. Sometimes, the death instinct is expressed directly, as in suicide, but more often indirectly by people deliberately choosing very high-risk activities like mountain climbing, or free-fall parachute jumping. Usually, however, life instincts override the death instinct. Energy is associated with these instincts; the energy associated with the death instinct is generally referred to as destructive energy, and the energy associated with the life instincts as *libido*.

In Freud's system, two basic drives are associated with, or are part of the life and death instincts – the sexual drive and the aggressive drive. Freud thought that the aggressive drive was not usually directed towards the person himself or herself, but, as it has energy and cannot be suppressed entirely, it is normally displaced onto objects or people in the environment. Freud was quite clear that, in his view, a tendency towards aggressive or destructive behaviour is a natural condition of humankind. To Rogers, there is only one motivational force behind human behaviour – the actualising tendency. In contrast to Freud, Rogers thought that this basic motivation is constructive, creative and positive.

Towards Fully Functioning

The idea that human beings have a natural tendency towards destructiveness is where Freud and Rogers would have disagreed most. In developing his theory of actualisation, Rogers looked to examples from the natural world that might indicate the existence of such a tendency. He observed that, wherever environmental conditions were favourable, organisms tended to become what he called 'fully functioning'. In other words, the innate characteristics of any organism, whatever they may be, become as fully realised as environmental conditions allow. Even where the environment is not ideal, or is even hostile to the organism involved, it still makes attempts towards growth and development. Short of death itself, an organism's actualising tendency cannot be destroyed, although it can only partially function in adverse conditions.

For example, a plant kept away from the light will still strive to grow, and will put out shoots that struggle towards whatever light source is present. Animals denied proper food will try to find whatever nourishment is available, and will still make attempts to reproduce, even though those attempts may be doomed to failure. In his book *A Way of Being* (Rogers, 1980), Rogers described these ideas:

> In short, organisms are always seeking, always initiating, always 'up to something'. There is one central source of energy in the human organism. This source is a trustworthy function of the whole system rather than of some portion of it; it is most simply conceptualised as a tendency toward fulfilment, toward actualization, involving not only the maintenance but also the enhancement of the organism (p. 123).

Events in the plant and animal worlds have their parallels in the world of people, though such parallels need to be viewed with some caution. Rogers' view was that from birth we are active seekers of fulfilment, and we are often far more consciously aware of this process than would be the case if it was an instinct in the way that term is applied to animals. Provided our environmental circumstances are favourable there is every chance that each human being will grow to express all of his or her potential, and Rogers thought this potential is invariably positive and constructive. In other words, whenever a person is freely able to choose from a number of alternative courses of action, some positive and some negative, the actualising tendency directs the person towards choices that are constructive and life-enhancing, rather than self-destructive. Rogers also believed that individual decisions, when guided by the actualising tendency, tend to be in the direction of both self and other-enhancing, a more obvious process when environmental conditions are supportive of the individual, and not hostile or threatening. Environmental conditions are not, however, limited to the presence or absence of nourishment, light and warmth, but include the relationships we have with each other and the values of the society or culture into which we are born.

The specific ways in which each of us attempts to actualise vary from one person to the next in any culture, and from one culture to the next. In ideal circumstances, the possibilities for creative and purposeful behaviour are immense, and people will choose different courses of action according to their own unique sets of preferences. However, while it is relatively easy to describe ideal circumstances in terms of nourishment, warmth, light and air, for example (in other words, the physical environment), it is not so easy to describe it in terms of the psychological environment.

The Psychological Environment

There are some elements to this psychological environment that must be present if individuals are able to experience their surroundings as conducive to growth and development. They are essentially concerned with the qualities of the relationships a person has, particularly (but not only) during early childhood. In other words, for the actualising tendency to operate on an individual level, there are certain psychological needs that must be met. If they are not, then just like the plant deprived of water or light, the individual will be denied the opportunity to become fully functioning.

The most important of these psychological needs is the infant's need for what Rogers termed 'unconditional positive regard'. Another way of putting this is far more simple: children need love. An infant's innate need is to experience *unconditional* love, the kind of love that will not be withdrawn if the infant should behave in ways that are unacceptable to those on whom it depends. This does not mean that *any behaviour* is accepted uncritically, but that the infant is continually treated as an individual of basic worth, even when behaviour is regarded by others as not acceptable. There is a real difference between saying to a child, for example, 'You are a bad person', and 'That was a bad thing to do'. The first focuses on the person of the child, the second on the behaviour.

Rogers' theory includes the idea that infants have an efficient means of discriminating between experiences that maintain and enhance themselves, and those that do the opposite. In this sense, the actualising tendency operates from the moment of a person's birth. Right from the start, the infant's valuing process is an internal one. He or she is not dependent on the evaluations of others in deciding between constructive and destructive alternatives.

Objective, scientific evidence for the existence (or otherwise) of an actualising tendency is, of course, hard to come by. It is difficult, if not impossible, to set up an experiment in controlled, laboratory conditions that would adequately test such a hypothesis. (The same is true for Freud's theories concerning the existence of *id, ego* and *superego,* or for the existence of *libido*.) However, one experiment does tend to support the existence, in infants, of an inherent ability to discriminate between foods that are needed to maintain and enhance life, and those that are not. In this experiment (Davis, 1928) three infants aged nine months, ten months and eight months were offered a range of foods, two of the infants for six months, and one for a year, from which they could choose freely. The foods included drinks (water and milk), various fruits and vegetables, grains and meat. Over a period of time it was found that the infants chose a healthy, balanced diet, although what they chose at any one meal was unpredictable, and sometimes surprising, for example four bananas or seven eggs at a single meal! The infants' appetites were good, none showed any signs of discomfort, abdominal pains or constipation, and all three children showed normal development in weight, bone development and general well-being. Although this and similar experiments have recently been criticised (Galef, 1991) they do provide some evidence that even very young children know what is best for them and are able to make choices in that direction.

Characteristics of the Fully Functioning Person

The specific ways in which people become more fully functioning vary from one person to the next, but there are some universal characteristics of this process. These include, for example, being open rather than defensive; relying more on one's own internal value system than on judgements made by others; being able to enter into and maintain close relationships with others; a concern for social issues rather than being self-centred, and having a flexible, changing attitude towards life rather than a fixed or dogmatic one.

Rogers supported his view that the actualising tendency is positive and constructive by reference to his work with people in counselling and psychotherapy. Whilst he saw many indications that people were engaged in a struggle to find more fulfilling ways of living, he could find none that led him to believe that people were *naturally* destructive or evil:

> I have little sympathy with the rather prevalent concept that man is basically irrational, and that his impulses, if not controlled, will lead to destruction of others and self. Man's behaviour is exquisitely rational, moving with subtle and ordered complexity toward the goals his organism is endeavouring to achieve. The tragedy for most of us is that our defences keep us from being aware of this rationality, so that consciously we are moving in one direction, while organismically we are moving in another (Rogers, 1957b).

'But', you may argue, 'isn't all this a bit idealistic? Don't people do the most terrible things to themselves and others? How can you believe the actualising tendency to be so positive and constructive in the light of all the war and violence that goes on all the time?' This is, of course, a very fair point. To respond to it, we need to go a step further and trace how, in person centred theory, actualisation involves the development of a self or self-concept, and how this self can work in ways that run counter to the general actualising tendency. How person centred psychology can propose that human beings are constructive rather than destructive, without denying the violent and aggressive behaviour we see almost everywhere, we discuss in the next two chapters.

In person centred psychology, in common with many other personality theories, early childhood experiences are considered very important. The single most important factor is the degree to which we experienced love and acceptance from significant others, usually (but not necessarily) parents. Rogers thought that children need to feel *unconditionally* loved and valued by people who are significant and important to them. The trouble is that love can be either conditional or unconditional. If love is offered unconditionally (with no strings attached), then children are able to be naturally expressive and accepting of all their feelings. Conditional love refers to love that is given only if the child behaves in approved ways, and, if the child behaves in ways that are unacceptable, then he or she risks love being withdrawn. The result is that the child begins to think of himself or herself in terms of the evaluations of others. Rogers' phrase for this was *conditions of worth*, and it refers to the ways in which our self-concepts are fashioned by the judgements of those around us. The unafraid person in our example above would have been loved and accepted for being fearless, but ran the risk of rejection for showing fear. As McLeod (1993) points out, the concept of conditions of worth constitutes the entirety of the person centred model of child development. In other words, there are no stages of development like there are in Freudian psychology.

In parallel with the need for positive regard from others arises a related need – that of positive self-regard. This refers to the view we have of ourselves as valuable or of worth. However, our view of ourselves is largely determined by the values we have absorbed (or introjected) from others, so in an effort to maintain self-regard, we tend to exclude from our self-concept any characteristics which have been labelled by others as unworthy. For example, take the case of someone who begins to feel anger towards a member of her family. If she has the introjected value that feelings of this kind are unacceptable, she will not be able to maintain positive self-regard if she were to allow these feelings to develop. As a result, she may try to deny her feelings or distort them into something more acceptable to her and congruent with her self-concept.

The Organismic Valuing Process

To understand this better, we need to introduce another concept from person centred theory – the idea of an *organismic valuing process*. Although the term itself is rather ungainly, the idea is quite simple. As infants, we start out in the world knowing what is good and not good for us. The yardstick we use to judge when to value something either positively or negatively is whether or not it contributes to maintaining or enhancing our development. This valuing process operates quite spontaneously; we do not put much thought into it. For example, when we are hungry we positively value being fed, and when we are no longer hungry we negatively value being fed. Positively valued experiences include being comfortable, being able to play, and being able to express our curiosity about the world that surrounds us. Negatively valued experiences include sudden movements or noises, nasty tastes and so on. Hjelle and Ziegler (1981) describe this as:

> In a sense, the organismic valuing process is a monitoring system that keeps the human infant on the proper course of need satisfaction. Infants evaluate their experiences according to whether or not they like them, whether they are pleasing or displeasing, and so on. Such evaluations result from their spontaneous responses to direct experiences, i.e., they are completely 'natural' (pp. 409–10).

Rogers thought that if we could continue functioning in this way throughout our lives, that is, trusting in our own internal valuing process, then we would be less prone to anxiety or other forms of psychological disturbance like depression or neuroticism. By the time we reach adulthood, however, most of us have become separated from our own 'internal guides', and we depend instead on the values we introjected as young children, believing them to be more reliable guides to our behaviour. Another way of putting this is to use the term *locus of evaluation*. If the locus, or source, of our evaluations lies externally to us, that is, in the beliefs and attitudes exhibited by others, we are no longer trusting of our own internal sources – our organismic valuing process.

The central concept in person centred personality theory is the *self*. We experience the world and the things and people in it, and we attach meaning to them. Part of what we perceive we separate out as 'me', or 'I', and our self-concept becomes established. Pervin (1989) makes two further points in connection with this person centred concept of the self:

> First, the self is not a little person inside of us. The self does not 'do' anything. The individual does not have a self that controls behaviour. Rather the self represents an organised set of perceptions. Second, the pattern of experiences and perceptions known as the self is, in general, available to awareness, that is, it can be made conscious (p. 181).

In addition, there is one further, related idea in Rogers' personality theory – that of the *ideal self*. The ideal self is the self-concept we would most like to have, and we may experience quite a gap between our current self-concept and our ideal self. The notion of an ideal self is highly consistent with Rogers' view that personality is not a static, once-and-for-all thing, but is always capable of change and development.

Another characteristic of the infant is his or her tendency towards actualisation, a trend that continues throughout life. As we saw in

Chapter 2, actualisation involves the inherent tendency of any organism to strive towards greater realisation of potential, and in the human infant, the need to actualise is expressed within the reality of the world as the infant experiences it.

Reality Is What We Perceive It To Be

What constitutes reality for us is dependent on how we perceive it. For example, if a 2- or 3-year-old is playing in the garden and a cat appears, the infant may perceive this as frightening or dangerous. Even though others know that the cat is harmless and playful, it is the infant's perception of the cat that guides his behaviour, not the 'reality' that the cat is harmless. However, the infant's relationship with his environment is not static, and if his continuing experience is different from his initial perception, then his perception is likely to change with time. This dynamic relationship with the environment, indicating that we are constantly taking in information, giving it meaning and perhaps adjusting our perceptions and behaviour accordingly, is directed by the actualising tendency. The primary motive in life is to maintain and enhance ourselves; to become all of whatever we are capable of becoming, and this involves us in being open to our experiencing.

Actualisation and Self-actualisation

The actualising tendency is, in person centred psychology, the sole motivation for human behaviour. The development of a self and a self-concept is a product or sub-system of the general actualising tendency. The terms *actualising tendency* and *self-actualisation* often get confused, but they do not refer to the same process.

Guthrie Ford (1991) makes the distinction much clearer:

> Like the actualising tendency from which it is derived, the tendency towards self-actualisation is also motivationally invested in maintenance and enhancement; *but* its particular function is to maintain and enhance the self-structure rather than the organism in general (pp. 23–24).

It is important to make this distinction between actualisation and self-actualisation, because it links together the other ideas we have discussed so far – those of the self-concept and incongruence particularly. It also explains how person centred psychology deals with an apparent (rather than real) logical contradiction. On the one hand, it proposes an actualising tendency as an inherent characteristic of human beings which motivates people towards positive, constructive and sociable ends. On the other hand, person centred psychology acknowledges that people's behaviour is often anti-social and destructive.

For the moment, however, let us assume that you are not an anti-social or destructive person, though like most people, you may very well experience occasional anti-social or destructive feelings. Your conditions of worth, and your internalised values, will lead you to believe that you are a certain kind of person with particular qualities, some good, some bad. This self-concept will be the self that you continually strive to actualise, choosing some courses of action and not others. It is important to realise that it is the conditioned self that is being actualised, not the true (or organismic) self. In this sense, the actualising tendency and the need to self-actualise are working against each other, and a state of incongruence now exists.

People with a self-concept that consists of many negative conditions of worth are likely to have low self-esteem. They are unlikely to value themselves very highly, or place much trust in their own experience or feelings. Behaviour will, therefore, be directed towards playing the part they have come to believe to be true about themselves. What they do will be a consequence of their internalised evaluations of themselves, perhaps as people of little worth, or little talent, or in some way unacceptable to others. As you can imagine, this becomes something of a self-fulfilling prophecy – if you believe yourself to be unacceptable to others, you are likely to behave in ways that are in accord with this part of your self-concept. The result will be that people are more likely to treat you as unacceptable, and this will tend to reinforce your self-concept.

Alternatively, the need for positive regard from others can be so strong that some people put aside their own needs and feelings, and behave in ways that are designed to attract positive regard. Sometimes, this behaviour can become quite self-destructive and unhealthy. Many of us are familiar with people who are always doing things for others, putting themselves in second or third place and valuing other people's feelings more highly than their own. Whilst a certain degree of altruism is an attractive and healthy quality, this can become unbalanced to such a degree that people begin to see themselves as of worth only to the extent that they are useful to others. This can be a strong condition of worth, and it can be just as unhealthy as the person who never considers others and seems totally self-centred.

A Case Study

How conditions of worth arise and become incorporated into the self-concept will be clearer if we look at a short case study. Although the subject of this study, Jake, is an imaginary figure, the things he says about himself are characteristic of people with many negative conditions of worth.

Jake is a 22-year-old man with a history of being in trouble with the police. He describes himself as quick-tempered, distrustful of others and impatient with his own feelings and those of others. His father is a drunken and violent man who has served several prison sentences for violent crimes. Jake's mother describes herself as someone who has always had to struggle, was never considered as important when a child, never encouraged to try and do well at school, or to make any kind of career for herself. Despite this, she has done her best to provide for her family and to show love and affection, but Jake's father is an angry man who sees displays of emotion as attempts to manipulate him.

Jake now thinks of himself as a 'no-hoper' who never has any luck. He remembers life at home as one of being in a constant state of fear; he never knew when his father would turn violent, just that it happened often. Jake's one attempt to make something of himself had failed, and he remembers his father being very scornful of this failure. Jake has gone on to commit several acts of house-breaking, but eventually was caught and put on probation. He is a member of a group of young men in a similar position, all of them petty criminals. Esteem and admiration of the group can be won by success at burglary and getting away with things, but Jake has failed here too.

In this example, we can see that Jake has internalised a number of negative conditions of worth. His father's attitude, that Jake is a failure and burden, has been communicated and emphasised over and over again. As a child, Jake would have received many messages concerning his lack of value, and the fact that he was no good at anything and unlikely to make a success of himself. Jake's self-concept would have included these beliefs about himself, though they might have been softened by his mother's more caring attitude. Jake's distrust of people, and his suspicion and impatience with feelings, are the result of experiencing his father's expression of feelings as violent. He cannot value feelings in any way other than as painful and destructive.

The self that Jake actualises in his relationships with others is determined by his internalised conditions of worth. They have left him with a negative view of himself as a person of little value. His low self-esteem means that he has little motivation in life, and has become resigned to being a 'no-hoper' for ever. Other people describe his personality as 'aggressive', 'uncaring' and 'anti-social'. To act in ways that are considerate or caring of others would be inconsistent with his self-concept. His way of self-actualising has become one of taking advantage of others, of attempting to manipulate them and trying to win esteem from his peer group by being a successful criminal.

Earlier, I said that as far as person centred psychology is concerned, personality is not rigid and unchangeable. It is possible for Jake to free himself of his negative conditions of worth, and to gain a sense of self-esteem and self-worth. Just like everybody else, Jake's actualising tendency is still available to him, though it has become buried under layers of conditions of worth. Although it might be very difficult for him, Jake could find relationships in which he feels valued and accepted without so many conditions. These relationships need not *approve* of Jake's destructive behaviour, or even find it remotely acceptable, but they might enable Jake to see beyond his conditions of worth, to the person underneath who is still in need of love and acceptance, and still capable of giving them to others.

It is even possible for Jake to do this for himself and by himself. It is not unknown for people to make quite radical changes in behaviour, attitudes, values and personality without any apparent help from outside. Though this is possible, it is more likely that if Jake can feel understood and not judged as worthless by at least one other person, he will become more trusting of himself and others, and more likely to change in ways that are more constructive and fulfilling for him. How person centred psychology offers help to people who are unhappy with themselves and who want to change, we discuss in Chapter 10, 'How Do Person Centred Therapists Help?'.

Chapter 4
If People Are So Constructive, Why Do They Do Such Destructive Things?

So far in this section, I have written very positively and optimistically about human nature and humankind's capacity for creative, constructive action. Yet I am very aware that there are countless examples of people behaving towards themselves and others that are anything but creative or constructive. A brief glance at any newspaper or TV news programme brings us shocking and horrific examples of humankind's capacity to be brutal, some might say 'evil'. How, then, can person centred psychology maintain that human nature is basically constructive and social and that the actualising tendency *always* operates in this direction?

Within humanistic psychology, this issue has been discussed many times, but one of the most informative of these discussions took place between Rollo May and Carl Rogers during 1982. Rollo May views people as 'an organised bundle of potentialities' (May, 1982), and has coined the term *daimonic*, by which he means, 'the urge in every being to affirm itself, assert itself, perpetuate and increase itself...'(May, 1969). May believes that:

> If the daimonic urge is integrated into the personality (which is, to my mind, the purpose of psychotherapy) it results in creativity, that is, it is constructive. If the daimonic urge is not integrated, it can take over the total personality, as it does in violent rage or collective paranoia in time of war or compulsive sex or oppressive behaviour. Destructive activity is then the result (May, 1982).

Rogers was very aware of people's destructive capacities. He had been working in psychotherapy for many years with individuals who had expressed violent, murderous thoughts and feelings, and some of those people had acted out their destructive feelings. In writing about Rollo May's contribution to humanistic psychology, Rogers had remarked:

For myself, though I am very well aware of the incredible amount of destructive, cruel, malevolent behaviour in today's world – from the threats of war to the senseless violence in the streets – I do not find this evil is inherent in human nature. In a psychological climate which is nurturant of growth and choice, I have never known an individual to choose the cruel or destructive path. Choice always seems to be in the direction of greater socialization, improved relationships with others. So my experience leads me to believe that it is cultural influences which are the major factors in our evil behaviours... So I see members of the human species, like members of other species, as *essentially* constructive in their fundamental nature, but damaged by their experience (Rogers, 1981).

Rollo May's point to Rogers, however, was that Rogers blamed culture for stimulating people's destructive behaviour. 'But', asked May, 'who makes up the culture except persons like you and me? ... who is responsible for this destructive influence and injustice, except you and me, and people like us? The culture is not made by fate and foisted upon us' (May, 1982). May believed that evil was present in the culture because the people who constitute it are themselves both good and evil: 'Our culture is partially destructive because we, as human beings who live in it, are partially destructive, whether we be Russians or Japanese or Germans or Americans.'

Finally, in the correspondence with Rollo May, Rogers expressed some of the similarities between himself and May, and described a situation in which destructive feelings had given way to more positive ones:

It is interesting that in our decisions about what to do about evil behaviour and evil situations, we seem remarkably similar. We take the best action we can to oppose evil, to destroy the causes, to try to reach people who are acting in hurtful ways. I am pleased I had the opportunity to work with groups composed of hostile and feuding individuals whose evil intentions toward one another were very evident. In a group we worked with from Belfast, which included both Catholic and Protestant extremists as well as moderates, a Protestant young woman said in one of the early sessions, 'If a wounded IRA man were lying before me on the street, I would *step* on him!' This was typical of some of the bitter feelings expressed. Yet in a climate of understanding and acceptance those people changed so much in attitudes in a short sixteen hours of contact that when they went back to Belfast they worked in teams of two to show the film to groups in the interest of reconciliation (Rogers, 1982).

Conditioning and Choice

Rogers tried to account for the evil behaviour so often observed in the world in terms of two elements – social conditioning and voluntary choice. He believed that every evil behaviour is brought about by varying degrees of these two elements:

I, and others, have had murderous and cruel impulses, desires to hurt, feelings of anger and rage, desires to impose our wills on others. It is well to
bear in mind that I also have a capacity to vomit for example. Whether I, or
anyone, will translate these impulses into behaviour depends, it seems to
me, on two elements: social conditioning and voluntary choice. Perhaps we
can use Hitler as an example. His early personal life and social circumstances certainly made it natural that he would try to fulfil himself by being
a big shot, a leader full of hatred toward those he perceived as responsible
for his humiliation. But beyond that, in acts like the decision to exterminate
the Jews, a personal choice for which he was responsible was also a very
real factor (Rogers, 1982).

The term 'social conditioning' can mean many different things. It
ranges, for example, from helping children learn how to play and to
relate to others, through to the invidious labelling of people, often in
infancy, as unacceptable or of little or no value. It is this process that
results in the incorporation of negative conditions of worth into the
self-concept. Rogers' choice of Hitler as an example is an obvious, but
still interesting one in this context. Hitler's early years have been
explored by Alice Miller, once a psychoanalyst but who has now
resigned from the international psychoanalytic community because of
her sharp disagreement with classical Freudian theory.

Alice Miller and Social Conditioning – the Case of Adolf Hitler

Miller has written extensively about an aspect of social conditioning
that she refers to as 'poisonous pedagogy', by which she means the various theories and practices of child rearing (e.g. Miller, 1983, 1984,
1987, 1990, 1992). It is these practices that Miller sees as resulting in
self-destructive impulses which can, under some circumstances, get
played out in society as acts of extreme destructiveness and violent
aggression. This idea is very close to Rogers' concept of conditions of
worth, but Miller goes much further than Rogers in describing specific
elements of social conditioning. In selecting the life story of Hitler as
an example, Miller argues that even the most evil and destructive of
people were once innocent and helpless children. Miller believes that
Hitler was often severely beaten as a young child by his brutal father,
and she quotes statements from Hitler's sister as evidence for this.
Miller's belief is that violent and destructive acts are often repetitions
of violent experiences in childhood, but by the time adulthood is
reached, the person is the initiator rather than the victim of these acts.
To identify with the victims would be to restimulate their own childhood torment, and so such identification is suppressed.
   Miller's concept of the infant as innocent is similar to Rogers' idea

that we are born with an organismic valuing process that seeks positive fulfilment of potential, and that the nature of humankind is not innately evil or destructive. In Chapter 2 we put forward the idea that the actualising tendency is constructive and social and that, in ideal environmental conditions, it will become expressed in these positive ways. In Chapter 3, we saw how negative conditions of worth result in the formation of a false or conditioned self, and that it is this false self that operates in the world. Alice Miller gives us more ideas about how conditions of worth (although she did not use the term) can result in the acting out of suppressed emotions, such as rage and humiliation. In Miller's system, this acting out has compulsive, even ritualistic elements.

To stay with Rogers and Miller for a moment longer, we can also see how close the two were in their ideas about how early emotional damage can be put right. In Miller's words:

> To beat a child, to humiliate him or sexually abuse him is a crime because it damages a human being for life. It is important for third parties also to be aware of this, since enlightenment and the courage of witnesses can play a crucial, life-saving role for a child. The fact that every perpetrator was once a victim himself does not necessarily mean that each person who was himself abused is bound later to become the abuser of his own children. This is not inevitable if, during childhood, he has the chance – be it only once – to encounter someone who offered him something other than pedagogy and cruelty: a teacher, an aunt, a neighbour, a sister, a brother. It is only through the experience of being loved and cherished that the child can ever discern cruelty as such, be aware of it, and resist it. Without this experience he has no way of knowing that there is anything in the world except cruelty; the child will automatically submit to it and, years later, when as an adult accedes to power, will exert it as being perfectly normal behaviour (Miller, 1990: 193).

In the next section, we take a closer look at how Rogers thought people could be helped to overcome early conditioning and return to a more constructive way of life. Rogers' idea of unconditional positive regard as an ingredient of this process is akin to Miller's idea that we need experiences of being loved and cherished. Both Rogers and Miller see the origin of evil behaviour lying in early childhood conditioning.

Thorne (1992) points out that, 'There is evidence that Rogers was not wholly satisfied with his own arguments in favour of man's essential trustworthiness despite the almost overwhelming positive data from his therapeutic experience.' Thorne goes on to say:

> In the response to Rollo May he admits that he finds 'a shocking puzzle' in the famous experiments by Stanley Milgram and Philip Zimbardo which demonstrated, in the first case, that 60 per cent of people were willing to turn up electric current to a voltage which they knew would kill others, and, in the second, that randomly assigned 'guards' and 'prisoners' were rapidly caught up in violent destructiveness which became life threatening (p. 80).

Nevertheless, Rogers did not deviate from his position that the actualising tendency was the only motivational force behind human behaviour, and that its direction was towards positive and creative outcomes. Various explanations for the occurrence of evil behaviour did not convince him that such behaviour was either innate or natural. The introjection of conditions of worth results in a corruption of the actualising tendency resulting, in turn, in a conditioned self that attempts to actualise in bizarre, violent or futile ways. Rogers often referred to his work as a psychotherapist in support of his view that the core of personality is positive, and it will be helpful at this point to take a brief look at one such case.

The Case of Mrs Oak

The point of view that 'the innermost core of man's nature, the deepest layers of his personality, the base of his "animal nature", is positive in nature – is basically socialized, forward-moving, rational, and realistic' (Rogers, 1989: 74) is, as Rogers said, 'revolutionary', and he did not expect this view to be accepted easily. Rogers thought that religion, the Protestant Christian tradition in particular, 'has permeated our culture with the concept that man is basically sinful' (p. 74). He also believed that Freud's legacy was a view of human nature controlled by instincts which would, if allowed free expression, have very negative and destructive consequences. This idea is so ingrained in our culture that even Rogers admitted that 'I have been slow to recognize the falseness of this popular and professional concept' (p. 75). He thought that the explanation for this lay in the fact that, in therapy, 'there are continually being uncovered hostile and anti-social feelings, so that it is easy to assume that this indicates the deeper and therefore the basic nature of man' (p. 75). It was a gradual process for Rogers to realise that these feelings 'are neither the deepest nor the strongest, and that the inner core of man's personality is the organism itself, which is essentially both self-preserving and social' (p.75).

In Rogers' eighth interview with Mrs Oak, she talks about her feelings of sexual disturbance, that she feels pretty bad and bitter, and that underneath it all she has murderous feelings. She doesn't want to be violent, but 'it's more like a feeling of wanting to get even' (p. 75).

Rogers thought that, 'Up to this point, the usual explanation seems to fit perfectly. Mrs Oak has been able to look beneath the socially controlled surface of her behaviour, and find underneath a murderous feeling of hatred and a desire to get even' (pp. 75–6). Later in her therapy (31st interview), however, Mrs Oak begins to feel that despite the bitterness and hatred, there are also much less anti-social feelings, and a deep feeling of having been badly hurt. She has no desire to act on her murderous feelings, in fact she dislikes and wants to be free of them.

Mrs Oak continues to explore this theme, and in her 35th interview, she describes much more clearly what she has come to discover about herself – that underneath the hurt and bitterness is a self that is positive, and without hate. Rogers believed that Mrs Oak is a good example of a person for whom, 'the deeper she dug within herself, the less she had to fear; that instead of finding something terribly wrong within herself, she gradually uncovered a core of self ... which was deeply socialised' (p. 83).

Rogers' belief in the essentially constructive and social core of a person's personality was strengthened by his encounters with clients like Mrs Oak and, of course, many others. In his discussion of what he felt he had learned from his clients, Rogers remarked that 'we have not an animal whom we must fear, not a beast who must be controlled, but an organism able to achieve ... a balanced, realistic, self-enhancing, other-enhancing behaviour ...' (p. 85).

Section II
Becoming a Person

This section is about who we feel we are, how we got to be that way in the first place, and how we might use more of our own resources more creatively. Many people think that childhood influences are so powerful in shaping our personalities that once we have grown up there is not much room for change. As we have already seen, person centred psychology takes a radically different view. Whilst early childhood experiences are very influential, change and development can occur throughout life, and it is possible to tap into this tendency towards change quite deliberately.

One of the ways of helping people change is through counselling, or psychotherapy, and Rogers is best known for his development of an approach he called client centred, and, later, person centred therapy. In fact, it was what Rogers learned about people from listening to them in therapy sessions that led him to develop his theories of personality and personality change. Only later did he and others look to see if what they believed to be true about individual change could also be applied in other settings. Because psychotherapy is such an important aspect of the PCA, much of the next section is concerned with it in one way or another.

At the top of each chapter in this section, you will find an extract from a real life therapy session that Carl Rogers conducted in England in 1983. I asked the client involved, Ms G., for permission to use the transcript of the session (which is also on video), and she generously agreed to this. I am using it because although this thirty minute interview raised a lot of issues that were very personal for Ms G., at the same time I feel she spoke for many of us, although, of course, the specific details of Ms G.'s life story are unique to her. At the back of this book, you will find the whole transcript, and this will give you a chance to see how the interview developed, and how Rogers tried to stay as close as he could to Ms G.'s feelings and thoughts without attempting to interpret them or diagnose her in any way.

Carl Rogers was fond of saying, 'If it's personal, it's universal'. At first, this appears a rather paradoxical statement. While it seems the more personally we speak about ourselves, the more unique and separate we become, at a different level, the opposite is true. Although Ms G. describes circumstances and feelings that are hers, the general human concerns she touches on are very much part of all our lives, 'What did I learn about myself from others when I was a child?', 'How is that learning still affecting the way I am, even though intellectually I see things quite differently now?', 'Can I free myself of those early influences?', and 'Can I become more able to act spontaneously in the world without becoming fearful or anxious?'

The themes that run through the chapters that follow lie at the heart of person centred psychology. Individuals are believed to be social and creative, or at least potentially so, although this can be hard to accept when we see around us every day examples of thoroughly destructive, even 'evil' behaviour. How we become who we are depends on many complex things, possibly including our genetic dispositions, but certainly including the experiences we have of the environment in which we live.

Chapter 5 is about values and how we develop a view of the world in which we value some things more highly than others. I suggest that it is a good idea to think about our valuing process, and to ask why it is that we hold on to certain views and values. Did we arrive at our values independently, or have we unknowingly absorbed much of what we believe to be true from the people around us?

In Chapter 6, I ask about free choice. Does it really exist, or is it an illusion? I suggest that 'freedom' might be as much to do with the way we give meaning to our experiences as it is to do with more obvious things like choosing a career, or choosing who to vote for, or where (and how) to live. I reject the notion that life is entirely determined for us by forces outside of our control, but I admit that free choice is limited partly by the 'givens' of life, and partly by our own self-defeating behaviour.

Chapter 7 examines questions about being in close relationships and how we can be intimate with others without losing our sense of who we are. I discuss how our early experiences affect the way we conduct our relationships when we get older and more independent. This chapter develops a very important concept in person centred psychology – conditions of worth. This is connected with how we feel about ourselves – our levels of self-esteem and self-worth. The view we hold about ourselves, whether we feel ourselves to be individuals of worth and value, or people of little worth, or somewhere in between, will profoundly affect our ability to enter into open and creative relationships with others. I also suggest that relationships can be made more satisfying if we can become more self-aware and understanding of ourselves and others.

Chapter 8 is about the goals we establish for ourselves, and I make the important distinction between the 'real self', and the 'conditioned self'. I discuss how we can find ourselves spending much of our time and energy trying to become the person others want us to be, rather than the person we really are. This touches on another central theoretical concept in person centred psychology – congruence. In this context, congruence is about living more authentically and with more openness to experience.

Chapter 9 goes further into the problems and rewards of close, intimate relationships. We see how closeness and intimacy are often thought of as both very desirable but also risky and difficult. I suggest that close partnerships, whether temporary or permanent, can be places for growth and development if we can allow ourselves to take the risks that are often involved in being open and vulnerable to another person.

Finally, in Chapter 10, I discuss how person centred psychology, through counselling and psychotherapy, offers help to people who are in distress or who want to become more aware of themselves and to live more openly and authentically. We see how person centred therapy has a deep trust in the process of actualisation, and in each person's ability to change and develop towards more satisfying 'ways of being'. This is not a book about counselling and psychotherapy, but, as I said earlier, the person centred approach was born in the therapy room, and many of its concepts and values are derived from experiences of working with individual people in this context.

Chapter 5
Where Do My Values
Come From?

Ms G.: ...I'm thinking about that time when I was in the children's home, it was a Catholic home. It was a convent and they used to say things like that, like you know, everyone's got this thing about pity yourself, that you should think about other people and that was so much around me at that time and I think I really learned it very well. (Later): I always feel guilty when I'm crying, you know, I always feel as though I'm not allowed to cry.

'People should always obey the law, even when they disagree with it.'

'Young people should respect their elders, and always do as they are told.'

'In time of war, you should join the forces and fight, whether you agree with the cause or not.'

You will recognise the above statements as values, with which you may or may not agree. We all hold values, things we believe to be true, and we believe that our values are our own, arrived at as a result of mature thought and judgement, but is this always the case?

A *value* is the preference for one course of action over another, or the preference for holding one particular belief when there are other options from which to choose. Rogers was mostly concerned with what he called *conceived values* and *operative values*, (a term he borrowed from Morris, 1956). Conceived values indicate that a choice is being made against an anticipated outcome of choosing one thing rather than another. The example Rogers gave of a conceived value was, 'honesty is the best policy' (Rogers, 1964). Another example is given by Ms G. at the top of this chapter, 'think of others before thinking of yourself'.

An operative value need not involve much thought – it is the value choice an organism indicates through its behaviour, like when a dog settles in front of the fire rather than by a draughty door.

As we saw in Chapter 2, infants are thought to have what Rogers called *an organismic valuing system*. For example, hunger and thirst are negatively valued, and food and milk are positively valued. But when the infant's hunger or thirst is satisfied, food and milk become negatively valued. Infants also value new experiences; they are constantly exploring and experimenting with the world around them, but when they have had enough for the time being, exploration becomes negatively valued.

Flexible Values in Infants

One of the characteristics of this value system is its flexibility. One moment, the infant values food and drink, the next he or she doesn't. At another time, the infant is full of curiosity, the next he or she values peace and quiet. Something is positively valued to the extent that, at that moment, it will enhance the infant's actualisation. The selection of one thing, and the rejection of something else, is not a cognitive or intellectual process, it is what Rogers called an organismic one.

A second important characteristic of this process is that the source of discrimination between one thing and another is clearly within the infant himself or herself. At this early stage, there is no external influence, nobody prompting, and nobody directing the infant towards some choices and away from others.

So far, so good – infants have internal, rather than external sources of evaluation, and can rely on their own 'in-built compass' for direction. Later, however, they become more easily influenced by the attitudes and values of people around them. They begin to build up a picture of themselves that equates with what is most likely to contribute towards their continued survival. This process ends up with the development of conditions of worth, and a very similar process is at work when it comes to the development of a value system.

What happens, then, as the infant grows through childhood to maturity? Instead of relying on this internal source of evaluation, the child learns that while some things in the environment are positively valued by others, other things are negatively valued, and a process of *introjection* gets under way. The child begins to abandon the internal source of evaluation, and instead starts to behave in ways that will ensure its continued survival by maintaining the approval of others on whom it depends.

An example might help here. At a certain point in our development (it varies a little from one person to another) we become aware of our sexuality. As children, we are naturally curious, and our organismic valuing system prompts us to explore what these new feelings mean. We begin to explore our bodies, and notice the differences between our own and those of the other sex. Some children are able to experiment with their sexuality through play, others may seek out 'naughty' books and magazines.

Suppose, however, that a child is discovered reading one of these books. If the parent, or other adult, reacts with shock and horror, and punishes the child for being 'disgusting', we have a clear case of an external value being imposed on the child. The child will, likely as not, introject the value that sex is not to be enjoyed for itself, even though at another level the child knows that sex is interesting and a natural part of being a person.

Internalising Values from the Outside

There are many examples of values being imposed on others, and, like conditions of worth, these values become internalised as if they were our own, freely and individually arrived at. For example, the value that says obedience to authority is always a good thing, or the one that says working with your brain is better than working with your hands, are examples of values that may have been seen as highly desirable by those around us, and as a result, we are likely to have adopted them as if we arrived at them by our own free will.

The kinds of values we have introjected are likely to be the same or similar to those in the immediate culture with which we are familiar. For example, in most parts of our culture, stealing is negatively valued, but elsewhere, amongst gangs of shoplifters, for example, stealing is positively valued. The same goes with acts of violence. Mostly, violence is negatively valued, but in some parts of our culture being violent is an admired quality, and likely to be positively valued.

It is inevitable, and necessary, for us to absorb and maintain some of the values operating in the society in which we live. Social living and social organisation could not continue to exist if there were no consensually shared values at all. Thus, most of us positively value education, though we may disagree about its form, and what, exactly, should be taught in school, and so on. The problem arises when we find we have adopted a set of values that does not accord with our 'organismic experiencing' of what is life-enhancing for us, both as individuals and as members of social groups.

By the time we are adults, most of us have developed a value system that has, in the main, been introjected from other individuals and groups, but which we continue to regard as our own. Put another way, we have reached a point where we have shifted almost entirely away from the situation where we were our own source of evaluation, to one where the source of evaluation lies outside of us. Because these values have been introjected from the outside, we have no real way in which we can discover what has most value for *us*. We continue to defend these external values because we have discovered that they win approval and acceptance from others. An important characteristic of introjected values is that they are held as fixed, and are rarely examined or tested against our own experience.

Because we have given up our own internal source of valuing and handed it over to others, we have lost contact with the ability to trust and value our own functioning and experience. But, and here lies the heart of the matter, our organismic valuing system goes on functioning, even though we may be only dimly aware of it, or not aware of it all. The deep unease or anxiety which many of us feel can sometimes be accounted for by the discrepancy that is occurring between what we know organismically, and what we have introjected.

In the extract at the top of this chapter, Ms G. says, 'I always feel guilty when I'm crying ...' This is a good example of how someone *organismically* knows how she feels. She was hurt, and is feeling that hurt now, in the present moment. Her whole being attempts to express that hurt, to communicate it to someone she hopes will understand and accept her and her feelings. But, at the same time, feeling sorry for herself conflicts with two internal processes. Firstly it conflicts with the condition of worth that she is not acceptable if she expresses herself in this way, and secondly, it conflicts with the introjected value that 'it is wrong to think of yourself when others are so much worse off'.

You can understand how powerful this introjected value is, and how much it stops Ms G. from fully expressing herself. We can be pretty sure that *intellectually* she knows it is OK to feel sorry for herself, and she most probably would not condemn others for feeling sorry for themselves. But when it comes to herself, her inner experiencing and her introjected values are in sharp conflict and she feels guilt as a result.

In the interview with Carl Rogers, Ms G. begins to feel that she is being prized as a person of worth, and as a result she begins to value the various aspects of herself. She refers to her own experiences, 'I was hurt and not considered', and later she begins to use this as a guide to her behaviour, 'I think I'll be me for a little while', rather than the values she was subjected to twenty or so years previously.

Reconsidering Values

Once this process is under way, that of referring to and trusting our own experience and senses, we are in a position to reconsider the values we once thought to be fixed, and make them our own or reject them as no longer part of us. This process is close to the original valuing process we experienced in infancy, but there is an added dimension. It is similar in that the source of evaluation is internal rather than external, and in that it tends to be more fluid and less dogmatic – our values can be reconsidered as our experience changes. The extra dimension is that, as adults, we have now accumulated a lot of different experiences. We can refer to these past experiences, as well as being open to what is novel in the present experience.

Friedman (1992) writes about the 'real' values that are operative in our lives, and that they are:

> ... brought into being through our ever-renewed decision in response to the situations we meet. These values become touchstones of reality for us. We carry them forward not as abstract principles but as basic attitudes, as life-stances that we embody and reveal in ever new and unexpected ways (p. 17).

We tend to think of the process of changing values and beliefs as a gradual one, and for the most part this is true. But there can be dramatic and sudden shifts in our values that take us completely by surprise, and this is further evidence that values are not fixed, but always open to change. Examples of this happening can be found among people who have been caught up in life-threatening situations, in wars or natural disasters, for example. They are often profoundly changed by these experiences, and find that what they once thought was valuable, no longer holds any appeal for them at all.

Carl Rogers put forward a theory – he called it a 'decidedly tentative hypothesis' (Rogers, 1964) – in which he tried to account for the more gradual processes I have described. First of all, he thought that human beings, in common with all other animals, are always seeking experiences that will achieve the maximum self-enhancement. They are at least potentially able to receive feedback from the environment to enable them to adjust and change their behaviour to achieve this. Second, he thought that achieving self-enhancement is dependent on the extent to which people are open to the experiences going on within them. Third, he thought that people can be helped towards being more open to their experience, by being understood and valued in a relationship that enables them to feel things without threat of rejection.

Bayne et al. (1994) have offered a useful set of questions to consider about values:

What are your main values?

Do you act on them?
Do you want to act on any of them more?
If you do, what will you do less of?
Do any of your values conflict with each other?
How do your values affect others? (p. 160).

But suppose you do become more open to experience, able to evaluate it without filtering it through learned values, and you do become more trusting of your own experience as a useful way to guide your behaviour. What might be the consequences for you? If people were to do this, would they not become self-seeking and selfish, interested only in their own enhancement, even at the expense of others?

To answer these questions, Carl Rogers referred to his clinical experience as a therapist. He found that when people are truly valued, and experienced the freedom to express themselves openly, common value directions emerged which seemed to have a universal quality to them. These values included things like disliking pretences or hiding behind masks, moving away from pleasing others as an end in itself, being more self-directed and autonomous, being sensitive to the needs of others, and valuing intimate relationships.

The values that Carl Rogers identified from his work with clients belong to the class, culture and times with which Rogers was familiar. Rogers can be criticised for assuming them to be universal when they were derived from a restricted sample of the world's population. These days there is much greater sensitivity to the value systems inherent in different cultures. For example, in some cultures autonomous behaviour, self-reliance and independence are not as highly valued as behaviour that is oriented towards the development and continuation of groups.

In a similar vein, Wood (1986) questions how far Rogers' concept of values can cope with very complex situations, and what happens when values are in conflict with one another:

> There are some four or five billion people in the world, more than 150 nation states in which many more cultures are intertwined. Cultural values are in conflict all over the globe. To settle many disputes, common values – which outweigh the values in conflict – must be found. If your neighbour has built a system on a value for 'development' and you have built your system on a value for 'ecology', his 'destruction of nature' will eventually conflict with your 'blockage of progress' unless a higher value can be found on which the two of you can unite. Does an ideal person with a mere existential outlook have the necessary diversity, anticipatory vision, and ability to integrate himself in a social context which may resolve such problems?

Rogers found from his clinical experience, however, that people tended to value experiences and situations that would be both self-enhancing, and enhancing of the lives of others. Constructive, creative, and, above all, social values took over from defensive, self-centred or egocentric, individualistic values. This is consistent with Rogers' theory of actualisation which, he thought, always tended to move individuals in the direction of constructive living in both individual and social terms.

Chapter 6
How Much Free Choice Do I *Really* Have?

Ms G.: 'Cos I feel I can't *let go of things like hurt and I* can't *let go of things like resentment...I want to, I want to let go of those things, but I don't know how, how to do that ...*

The issue here is, how far you are free to choose, and how much is life determined for you by some combination of genetic characteristics, particular experiences and environmental factors?

Person centred psychology operates on the principle that while there are many obstacles and limitations to freedom, people can at least make the attempt to transcend them. Humankind is responsible for whatever it has become because people can choose from a number of alternatives of 'how to be', an exercise in freedom unique to humankind. Each individual is responsible for constructing meaning from experience, and therefore is the architect of his or her unique reality.

The Courage to be Free

To be one's own creator in this sense takes courage, because most of us fear the consequences and responsibilities that such freedom brings. To accept that all our values and projects are a result of our own free choice means we have to take sole responsibility for them. This brings a paradox with it – while we desire freedom we are also afraid of it.

Take, for example, a young person faced with a difficult choice. She has done well at school, and has three good 'A' levels. Everyone expects her to go to university and study economics with a view to getting a good job and becoming successful. However, she is also a very creative person, but to try to become an artist would be very risky, and it is by no means certain that she will be successful. Taking economics at university seems the safer option.

Will she follow her feelings and try to become an artist, or will she take the more predictable route? She knows that she will never be truly happy working in an office, but she also knows this will provide her with some security. Whichever choice she makes, she understands that she will have to live with the consequences, and that no-one can take responsibility for her. She won't be able to blame anyone if it turns out she has made the wrong choice.

If this young woman has wise and supportive parents or friends, they will help her assess the pros and cons of both decisions, but they will leave the final choice to her. What often happens is that people look back and discover that they allowed themselves to be too influenced by others, or that they went along with others' expectations of them, only to discover too late that they had made the wrong decision.

Making Choices

Making a genuine choice for oneself can be very hard to do. Sometimes it seems better or easier to go along with what is expected, even when we feel it is wrong for us. According to person centred theory, the capacity to choose is enhanced by being in relationships in which we are able to explore all the options freely. Ideally, these relationships would occur naturally for us in our everyday lives, but the reality for a lot of people is that such relationships are few and far between.

This is where counsellors and therapists can be of help. They can provide relationships where we can experience being accurately understood, respected and valued. Under such conditions:

> ...the client moves gradually toward a new type of realization, a dawning recognition that in some senses he chooses himself ... The client begins to realise, 'I am not compelled to be simply the creation of others, moulded by their expectancies, shaped by their demands. I am not compelled to be a victim of unknown forces in myself' (Rogers, 1961).

At first Ms G. talks about her fear that she is stuck with certain feelings that will never leave her: 'I *can't* let go of things like hurt ...'. Most of us probably recognise this, the thought that there are some things from which we will never be free, but as the counselling relationship continues, Ms G begins to get an inkling that change in this respect is possible, that she *can* begin to do something about it.

Rogers and Skinner

The opposing point of view – that humankind is genetically predisposed to react to environmental factors in particular ways – was well articulated by the late Dr B.F. Skinner. Skinner was responsible for the development of the theory of 'operant conditioning', a branch of behaviourism.

In a dialogue with Carl Rogers (Kirschenbaum and Henderson, 1989b) Skinner remarked:

> There is this strange feeling that if you deny the individual freedom or deny an interpretation of the individual based upon freedom and personal responsibility that somehow or other the individual vanishes. This is not at all the conclusion one could arrive at. I think you can make the assumption that each person is completely determined to do what he is now doing and is going to do by his own genetic and environmental history (p. 93).

For Skinner, while each individual is a unique combination of genetic factors and environmental influences, nevertheless what any particular individual does is not a matter of free choice, which Skinner regarded as an illusion, but an inevitable outcome of those combined factors. Even in matters of aesthetics, or appreciation of the arts and literature, it is positive reinforcement which is the determining factor, rather than any sense of free choice. In the same dialogue, Skinner went on to say:

> There is reasonable certainty, on the basis of evidence available now, that the extent to which a person enjoys music or art or literature, or the extent to which a person continues to work with a high level of interest in a given field – these things can be traced to lucky histories of reinforcement (p. 98).

Rogers had a paradoxical view of the question of free will and determinism. While he certainly believed in the existence of free choice, and that exercising it is not only possible but desirable, in his scientific work he proceeded from the point of view that humankind is determined by a combination of environmental and genetic factors. As a scientist, Rogers took advantage of the scientific method that proceeds on an 'If ..., then ...' basis: If I do so-and-so, then these things will happen as a consequence.

In his dialogue with Skinner, Rogers said:

> I am in thorough agreement with Dr Skinner that, viewed from the external, scientific, objective perspective, man is determined by genetic and cultural influences. I have also said that in an entirely different dimension, such things as freedom and choice are extremely real (p. 132).

Rogers believed that the deterministic approach is acceptable when it comes to conducting scientific experiments or observations, in that it is a method that helps to manage and control the experimental situation, but that it is not the whole picture. When you start to include considerations to account for more of the complexities of human behaviour and experience, you realise that human behaviour is not so easily predicted or explained. Friedman (1992), from a different standpoint, agrees with this somewhat paradoxical view:

One of the classic problems of 'human nature' is that of 'free will' versus 'determinism'. Transposed into the realm of psychology, it becomes the much more fruitful problem of personal freedom and psychological compulsion. The reality of unconscious compulsion makes it impossible to assert the existence of full, conscious freedom. But it is equally impossible to reduce man to a purely deterministic system. Human existence – in the well person as in the ill – is a complex intermixture of personal freedom and psychological compulsion, a paradoxical phenomenon that can be understood only from within (pp. 125–6).

Both Rogers and Skinner used the word *conditioning*, though in different ways. Skinner thought that the choices we make today are inevitably determined by everything that has gone before. Rogers thought that early conditioning could be overcome, and real choices could be made. But it would be a mistake to think of freedom only in terms of the freedom to do things, or go places, or possess material goods – in other words only to think of freedom as existing externally to us. This is not to say that these things are not important, but we need to complete the picture by considering a different kind of freedom.

An Expanded Definition of Freedom

For Carl Rogers, this expanded definition of freedom was:

> ...essentially an inner thing, something which exists in the living person quite aside from any outward choice of alternatives which we so often think of as constituting freedom. I am speaking of the kind of freedom which Victor Frankl vividly describes in his experience of the concentration camp, when everything – possessions, identity, choice of alternatives – was taken from the prisoners. Months and even years in such an environment showed only that 'Everything can be taken from a man but one thing: the last of human freedoms, to choose one's own attitude in any given set of circumstances, to choose one's own way (in Kirschenbaum and Henderson, 1989b: 84).

It is typical of Rogers that he should have seen 'freedom' as much in terms of 'inner life' as in terms of external circumstances. This goes to the heart of person centred theory – that who we are is a result of how we have interpreted and given meaning to the experiences we have had. The choices we made in the past were the best ones we could make at the time, given the need to survive, but this does not mean we have to stick to those choices for ever, or that we cannot change our feelings about ourselves.

The problem here is that we are likely to have distorted some of our experiences, or defended ourselves against them because to admit to their reality might threaten our self-concept, including its conditions of worth. Freedom, then, means that we are able to experience things without distorting them or changing them to fit what we think we need. Freedom comes from the ability to make choices from all the options available, not just those that fit with the expectations and values of others. To exercise freedom in this sense implies a more accurate and complete picture of ourselves, our values and our needs.

Freedom of choice is constrained both by external factors and by how much we need to deny or distort our experiences. Victor Frankl illustrated to Rogers how he was able to deal with the terrible things that happened. He knew that, ultimately, he did retain the freedom to choose the way he acted and reacted and the way he derived personal meaning from his experiencing.

Chapter 7
Can I Love Somebody, and Still Be Myself?

Ms G.: ... I feel OK about meeting people and ... spending a little bit of time with them ... but there's always a point where I want to run away and I think a lot of the time I do ... when it feels like it's getting too close.
Carl: So you like to go a little ways in meeting them but there's some point when you feel, 'No ... now we would really meet if we went any further', and you'd like to run away.
Ms G.: Yes ... and ... I'm thinking it's funny, it's ... I'm not afraid of what it is in you ... I'm afraid of what it is in me and, it's like in a way that I can con myself about what's in me if I don't meet with you, if I meet with you I have to give you something of me.

Close and loving relationships enable us to become intimate with other people. It is probably the case that almost everybody would prefer to be in such a relationship at some time in their lives. It is a sad fact, however, that many relationships (though by no means all) that start off with such high hopes, end in unhappiness.

Intimacy Can Be Risky

The paradox is that, while most people seek out (or at least long for) closeness and intimacy it can feel very risky and bring with it the fear that we will become very vulnerable. We risk being rejected and exposing aspects of ourselves to others that we may not like about ourselves. We also risk discovering things about ourselves that we would prefer remain undiscovered.

We have already seen how conditions of worth can, and often do, affect the way we relate to people as adults, even though the things we learned about relationships were learned mainly when we were very young. Early relationships act as models for us, and we bring those models to all subsequent relationships. The ways our parents related to us, the messages we learned about the rights and wrongs of relating, and the things we have come to expect from relationships all affect the way we form and maintain relationships when we become adults.

One of the reasons people give for relationships not working out is that they feel they cannot be themselves, that they are expected to change to suit somebody else's needs, rather than their own. They feel stifled or restricted rather than encouraged to develop in ways that feel right for them. People feel that if they are to continue with their relationship, they will have to give up part of themselves because it seems expected of them, and this, naturally enough, makes them feel incomplete and frustrated.

Expectations about roles and responsibilities can become very destructive. The idea, for example, that men should be strong and dominant within relationships, and that women should be passive and provide the caring and nurturing, may be changing, but there are still enough stereotypes remaining to make it difficult to know whether we are being a certain way because we want to be, or because it is expected.

A Case Study

Carl Rogers (1973) gave an example of a marriage between Jennifer and Jay that appeared idyllic from the outside, but in reality became unhappy and destructive. Before marriage, Jennifer had been a creative and self-directed person, getting new ideas and working on them successfully. Once married, however, she adopted a 'back seat' supporting role to her new husband. She put herself and her needs second, and gave in to doing things his way. This, she thought, was what being married meant.

Jay was a successful professional, popular with his colleagues, and a good father to their two children. In their social circle, Jennifer was left on the outside, being a good hostess, but not really taking part. Gradually, she built up resentments towards her situation and to her husband, but was unable to express them openly. Although apparently capable and competent, Jay was in reality, very dependent on Jennifer to make important decisions. Jennifer began to resent this too, until the time came when she hated to hear him arrive home from work.

Jennifer became more and more depressed until she reached the point of contemplating suicide. Luckily, she sought help, and after a while was able to voice her anger and resentments, but it was too late to save the relationship. Jay was simply unable to understand what had happened and what had gone wrong for Jennifer.

This is a situation that might have been different had Jennifer not given up an important part of herself because she thought this was what she should do. Had she been able to express her resentments and mounting anger towards Jay more openly earlier, something could, perhaps, have been done. Jay also could have acknowledged that the competent professional face he presented was only part of the picture. The other part was the almost child-like dependence he had on Jennifer to help him make decisions.

Entering into an intimate partnership may bring with it some sacrifices, or at least some changes in our way of life, but sacrifices do not have to include the giving up or suppression of important parts of ourselves. The notion that intimacy must involve such suppression is, however, a widespread one. There often does not seem to be the concomitant realisation that intimate partnerships are where personal growth and change can be mutually enhanced and encouraged. This is connected with the idea that change is risky, which it is.

Personal Change and Self-discovery

Personal change involves a process of self-discovery, trying to get closer to our innermost feelings. There is a rich and complex variety of them, and some may seem unacceptable to us, let alone to others. To risk experiencing feelings that seem unpredictable, and to express them to someone else can seem an impossible task. We risk rejection and the withdrawal of love, and this can appear too high a price to pay. It seems better to sit on our feelings, rather than let them out. But all the time we deny our own feelings, or deny them suitable expression, we are suppressing parts of ourselves, and not giving ourselves opportunities to learn and grow.

Being aware of our feelings is only the first important step. The second is to accept ourselves for who we really are. The more we can own and accept ourselves, including those parts that are most difficult to accept, the more of a complete person we can be to live with and relate to. What seems dangerous is the relative unpredictability of this process. We can experience subtle pressure from others not to change, to stay the same predictable person we always were. Change can be an uncomfortable process to ourselves as well as to others, and partners can become bewildered and threatened by changes they see happening if they do not understand them.

Change involves giving up pretences and moving away from the defences that prevent us from being completely who we are. Defences involve the denial or distortion of feelings and experiences, but they are there for the very good reason that we learned that to admit certain feelings, or follow our intuitive way of being, risked the withdrawal of love and care by those on whom we depended. The man who tries to maintain the illusion that he is always strong, always in complete control and never afraid of anything, for example, often finds it difficult to admit to his need for tenderness, and that he is sometimes afraid and vulnerable. To begin to express his own tender, loving and nurturing side without feeling it as a challenge to his idea of what a man should be may be very difficult for him. To be able to do this means a shift away from being dependent on others for approval, to a greater confidence in his own judgement about himself and about what is right and wrong for him.

Communication

A recurring theme throughout this book is *communication*. We have already seen the important part played by good communication in a number of situations, but we need to return to that theme now because as far as intimate partnerships are concerned, communication can, as you would expect, make all the difference between success and failure. First of all we need to acknowledge that communication can be used to deny ourselves, to present a facade or false picture and to avoid intimacy, as much as it can enhance and deepen our relationships. If we are maintaining a false self, whether consciously or unconsciously, our communication will not be congruent with what is true about us at a deeper level.

Although there are no guarantees, our relationships are more likely to be satisfying if we resolve to move away from being defensive and guarded, towards being more open and honest with ourselves and each other. Relationships are more likely to be successful if we can communicate our feelings, and if we can endeavour to understand the feelings of others. A most important thing is the ability to communicate persistent feelings, those which last for a period of time, in a way that owns and takes responsibility for them, rather than blaming our negative feelings on someone else.

Sex and Sexuality

An area where relationships often find themselves in some difficulty is the whole area of sex and sexuality. Sexual feelings and behaviour are subject to more myths, taboos and injunctions than just about any other form of human experience. Adults often take destructive feelings about sex derived from childhood experiences into their later relationships. Although loving someone does not necessarily imply the need for a sexual relationship, sex does form an important part of many intimate adult partnerships. The discovery, exploration and sharing of sexual feelings can be both exciting and full of danger. Difficulties in relationships often show up first, or most dramatically in sex, and it is important that sex does not get blamed for difficulties elsewhere in the relationship. Sex, apart from anything else, is (or can be) a particularly intimate form of communication, and this is why problems with intimacy and communication often show up in sexual behaviour.

You can be forgiven for thinking that good sex is simply a matter of technique, particularly given the flood of sex manuals and videos that are available these days. Whilst these things can be helpful in overcoming ignorance or embarrassment, sex is part of our 'way of being', not a technique to master. Below is an example of how sexual difficulties became the focus of attention in a relationship where deeper problems were elsewhere. The example is of a heterosexual relationship, but its general lessons are just as appropriate to gay relationships.

A Second Case Study

John and Susan had been together for about two years. They loved each other, and were often very close, but they had not been able to have a very satisfactory sexual relationship. John was often very anxious when it came to sex, and Susan was left, more often than not, feeling that sexually she was not very attractive to John, though nothing could have been further from the truth. Both had a real difficulty in talking about sex, and very rarely attempted to talk. John's anxieties stemmed from his feeling that women were not interested in sex, and that sex was something a man did to a woman which she tolerated rather than enjoyed.

Susan was rather ashamed of her strong sexual feelings. She associated them with 'loose' women, something she had learned from her parents, who were very Victorian in their sexual attitudes. She learned how to suppress her sexuality, believing that if she gave in to it, John would no longer love and care for her. The reality was that both John and Susan wanted a fulfilling sexual relationship, but neither understood how the other felt about sex, and neither was prepared to risk opening up on the subject. They began to see their 'problem' as a sexual one, rather than as a problem of trust, openness and communication. When they were helped to become more open in their communication generally, they began to feel more confident in sharing their sexual needs and feelings. Eventually, John became less anxious and Susan began to enjoy her strong sexual feelings.

Partnership is a Process, not a Fixed Contract

A partnership in which communication is valued and worked on is, as Carl Rogers (1973) said, a continuing process, not a fixed contract. The process element of a partnership means that each person is free to grow and develop in his or her own way, in other words to become more of who they can be, whilst learning to appreciate the other person as he or she grows too. Here, we have reached the central paradox of the question at the top of this chapter – 'Can I love someone, and still be myself?'. Now we are coming to the point where we could ask the question differently, 'Can I love someone, and not be myself?'

Person centred theory and philosophy consistently takes the view that people are forward moving, creative and social. Elsewhere I have written in more detail about the actualising tendency, and how this tendency can find expression in each individual, even though people may have been very damaged and hurt by their experiences. In this context, as in all others, actualisation involves the continuing movement of each person towards becoming more 'fully functioning'. Carl Rogers thought that partnerships in which one or the other person loses unique identity, giving it up as it were, with the idea that this will lead to a form of 'togetherness' are unlikely to endure for long. On the other hand, partnerships in which both people are enabled to establish their separate identities and to express themselves as valued individuals are likely to be emotionally more stable and satisfying. However, Rogers also pointed out that people can sometimes grow away from each other, as well as towards each other, and that the growth and development of one person can be threatening to the continuation of a relationship.

The ideal situation is where both partners are able to develop and change, each in his or her unique way, and where both partners are able to view the growth of the other as something to be welcomed and valued. As we have already seen, this might mean having the courage to move away from culturally expected patterns of behaviour and relating, or taking the time to determine how far we subscribe to expectations as a matter of free choice. The notion that you need to give up part of yourself in order to enter into a loving relationship with another person is a dangerous one. If the part you give up is simply suppressed, it is likely to lead to resentment and anger later.

Chapter 8
What Do I Want From Life?

Ms G.: I think perhaps I was trying to be somebody else ... trying to be what other people wanted me to be, I think. I think it's all part of them not considering me ... how they want me to be ... I think I'll be me for a while.

Parents, when asked what they want from life for their children, often reply that, above all, they want their children to be happy. Happiness seems to be one of the most desirable things in life, but all too often, achieving it turns out to be elusive. If we were to believe what we read, hear and see on TV and in the newspapers, we could be forgiven for believing that happiness comes only through money, fame or success.

There seems to be a strong cultural belief that there is a meaning to existence, even though most of us do not know for sure what it is. Person centred psychology takes the view that the decision about what is and what is not meaningful in life is ours to make, but it is not easy. This is quite different from some religious philosophies where what is and what is not meaningful is more or less clearly described. We also grow and change, so that what might appear to be meaningful (and make us happy) one day, does not always stay the same. The many messages we get about what is and what is not worthwhile, and how we should think, feel and behave can get so confusing that it seems impossible to come to our own conclusions based on our own experiencing.

The Struggle Between Two 'Selves'

I have already described how in each of us are two 'selves' – the organismic self and the conditioned self. The organismic self is motivated by the actualising tendency, and the conditioned self by the need for positive regard. As long as the needs of the organismic self are not being satisfied, we adopt coping strategies or defence mechanisms to compensate, and we defend the position of the conditioned self as this is the part of us of which we are aware. Our need for positive regard

means we constantly seek it out, usually from people who are important to us, whilst keeping the demands of our inner selves at bay.

When we live this way we are thought to be in a state of incongruence. The conditioned self is pursuing goals aimed at satisfying the
need for positive regard, which may not be the same as the needs of
the organismic self. One aim of person centred psychology is to find
ways of helping people to become more congruent. If the needs of the
organismic self can be brought into awareness then they can be understood and acted on. To do this, we have to challenge the needs, attitudes and beliefs of the conditioned self, and allow the needs of the
organismic self to be taken seriously.

Challenging the needs of the conditioned self can mean that many
emotions start emerging into our awareness, and it is likely that some
of these will be uncomfortable or painful. Fearing hurt, we naturally try
to suppress potentially painful feelings, but if we are to become more
congruent, all of our emotions need to be experienced so that we
know the part they play in making us who we are. Becoming more congruent means we can be more self-reliant, less dependent on reassurance from others, and we need to spend less energy and time on
maintaining the defences of the conditioned self.

We stand a better chance of being happy, or at least getting more of
what we really need from life, the more congruent we can be. We will
be less dependent on others and able to explore more of whatever
leads to positive self-regard. But paradoxically, there is a social expectation to conform to and obey society's rules, and the idea that by doing
this we will be happy, healthy and successful. For many people, however, this is simply not the case, and conforming to expectations from
others leads to a sense of dissatisfaction and unhappiness.

A Case Study

Emma was an intelligent and capable person, who really wanted a
career for herself. She did well enough at school, but she left when she
was sixteen because, in her family, education was considered to be for
boys. Girls, it was said, would be happiest making a home and becoming mothers. On leaving school, she trained for a while as a nurse (perhaps attempting to fulfil the nurturing and caring expectations of her).
She gave up nursing, however, when she got married and started to
have children. Emma never found being a mother fulfilling enough for
her, although she enjoyed much of it. She often felt depressed and
resentful, and this would spill over into angry outbursts. At forty years
of age, her husband left her and her children left home. She had never
been happy or content as a married woman bringing up children, but
the people around her could never understand this. She had a good
home, nice children, a good husband – what more could she want?

Emma really blamed herself for her marriage breaking up. She thought it was her fault for not being able to cope with the expectations that she had grown up to believe were so important. She found herself more or less alone, but discovered that she still had the ability to make a new life for herself. She went to evening classes, developed an interest in magazine production and desktop publishing and started a small company producing newsletters and publicity material for charities and small businesses. She now felt able to make decisions for herself and was using her intelligence and abilities creatively, and she felt better about herself and happier with life. As a direct result, she began to make better relationships with her children, become closer to them and more able to understand them.

Emma is an example of someone who faced a serious crisis in her life, and came through it more determined to listen to her own needs, and be guided more by her own values. Person centred psychology works on the principle that where people are able to become more congruent, and consequently more 'fully functioning', they become more positive about themselves, and are able to build better relationships with others as a result. Each person varies in what constitutes constructive and creative living for them. For some, it will involve a strong family life and a good job, for others it will involve having many relationships and never getting settled in one place or with one activity. The important thing is that the needs of the organismic or 'real' self are being expressed, rather than the need to live up to the expectations of others.

Characteristics of Congruence

Carl Rogers was not in the business of determining what constituted a good or happy person, but he did describe some ways in which he saw people develop as they became more congruent. He thought, for example, that the more congruent a person is able to be, the more able they are to value themselves, and believe in their self-worth. Similarly, such people see life more as a process than something fixed – they expect change to happen and are not threatened by it. What they want out of life is governed by a trust in their own experiencing, and they are able to resist pressure to conform to the expectations of others.

Simply having personal happiness as a goal seems, however, to involve a rather restricted view of life, and even a lack of empathy or understanding for others. It is a very individualistic line to take, and person centred psychology has been criticised for concentrating on the needs of the individual, whatever they may be, at the expense of the needs of society in a wider sense. Because there are so many injustices in the world, our personal happiness has to be seen in the context of the widespread unhappiness of so many others. Per~ chology is not, however, as 'individualistic' as it i~ assumed to be.

Social action and social change are as much a part of perso~ philosophy as individual change. Elsewhere in this book you wi~ examples of how the PCA attempts to initiate and influence change ~ different social contexts, but the common factor is the presence of people who highly value understanding and open communication. Embarking on a process of personal change often, if not always, leads to a greater empathy for others, and an increasing desire to become fully involved in life. The tendency towards 'navel contemplation', introspection and withdrawal from life is the exception rather than the rule.

For many people, a sense of fulfilment, belonging, or being socially creative, are better words than 'happiness' to describe personal goals in life. This does not, of course, mean that there is anything wrong with being happy or contented. When Ms G. says, 'I think I'll be me for a while', she is expressing the thought that up until this point she has found herself more concerned to be the way others want her to be, rather than discovering her own needs and being the person she really is. For all of us, fulfilment in life will be more possible if we can distinguish between our conditioned self and our 'real' self. Happiness and contentment are more likely to follow if what we do is a result of self-aware choices we make, rather than decisions determined by our conditions of worth.

The term 'fulfilment' is not, however, a very accurate one because what is experienced as fulfilling will vary from one person to the next, and from one culture and time to the next. Rogers' favoured term 'the good life' is equally problematic, and open to a variety of misinterpretations. However, Rogers clarified what he meant by the 'good life', first by saying what it was not, and then by saying what it was:

> It is not, in my estimation, a state of virtue, or contentment, or nirvana, or happiness. It is not a condition in which the individual is adjusted, or fulfilled, or actualised. To use psychological terms, it is not a state of drive-reduction, or tension reduction, or homeostasis (Rogers, 1961: 186).

Rogers believed that all these terms were used in ways that implied that their achievement meant that the person's goal in life had been achieved. The problem Rogers had with these terms was that they described a fixed state of being, whereas he consistently thought of life as a continuing process. Rogers' idea of 'the good life' is best summed up in his own words:

> The good life is a *process*, not a state of being.
> It is a direction, not a destination.
> The direction that constitutes the good life is that which is selected by the

total organism, when there is psychological freedom to move in *any* direction.

... So I can integrate these statements into a definition which can at least serve as a basis for consideration and discussion. The good life, from the point of view of my experience, is the process of movement in a direction which the human organism selects when it is inwardly free to move in any direction, and the general qualities of this selected direction appear to have a certain universality (Rogers, 1961: 186).

It is this 'process quality' of life that was so important to Rogers, and which became an integral part of person centred philosophy. It stands in stark contrast to philosophical views of the person which hold that 'human nature' leads us to take easy options, or that humankind is irrational and destructive. The 'good life', as described by Rogers is no soft option. It involves living with more intensity, and being more engaged with life in ways that allow for a greater range of experiencing.

When viewed in this way, the question, 'What do I want to get out of life?', becomes an existential one. The extent to which we are able to respond to each new experience without defence or distortion, governs the extent to which we can allow our 'self' and our personality to grow from experience. If we distort or 'edit' our experiencing to fit a preconceived notion of our self-structure, then that self-structure will remain fixed. The discovery of what we want becomes inextricably bound up with the discovery of who we are.

Chapter 9
Why Are Relationships So Important?

Ms G.: I just realised something ... part of the hurt is about not being considered, and I'm talking about when I was young and my parents kept on getting back together again and separating and getting back together again and separating and I went into children's homes and all sorts of things, that I wasn't considered. And now what I'm doing is not considering myself, I'm not ... it's like I can't consider myself, and I don't think that I'm important enough to be considered.

Carl: That childhood experience of being shuttled around and not really considered in the situation ... er ... resulted in you not being able to consider and take care of yourself ... (pause) ... and you must have felt very keenly the business of being treated as an object, just put here, put there and not really, not really considered, not really cared about.

Ms G.: I mean, how can you say what you want when you're four?

Generally, psychologists agree that our adult behaviour, feelings, expectations, and most of all, our sense of self-esteem or self-worth, are shaped by our experiences in childhood. A very important time is when we are at our youngest and most vulnerable, when we are dependent on others for our continued survival. The relationships we first have, with our parents or other primary carers, are usually the most significant. In the example taken from the interview with Ms G, we see that one of her early experiences was that she was not considered as important enough to be taken into account when decisions were being made that affected her life. This made it difficult for her to value herself as a person in her own right, an experience that deeply affected her.

People are social beings. Most of us are dependent to some degree on others to make life interesting and worthwhile. We are continually forming, building and ending relationships, and how successful we are at that depends a good deal on what we learned about ourselves during our very early years.

The Need for Positive Regard

An important aspect of our early experience concerns the degree to which (and how) we were loved. We have already seen how, as children, we needed positive regard from others, and that we also needed to develop self-regard. It follows that what we learned about ourselves from our earliest relationships will affect us for the rest of our lives. If we were fortunate, our early experiences resulted in a positive sense of self-worth – we value ourselves and trust our own experiencing. But, for many of us, childhood consisted of instances, perhaps a lot of them, when our individuality was denied or disapproved of in some way. When some childhood emotion was met with disapproval, or the threat of, or worse still, the actual withholding of love, we are likely to have repressed, or denied that emotion whenever it arose again. We learned we are only safe and loveable *on condition* that we think, feel and behave in ways that others demand of us, even when those conditions contradict our natural inclinations.

The Beginnings of Conditions of Worth

We were born into the world without values or belief systems. We were spontaneous – when we felt hungry we expressed it in the best way we could, and when that hunger was satisfied we were content. When we were in some other state of discomfort, we communicated it openly. We were being *fully congruent* – we knew what we felt, and we expressed it without 'editing'. It was when our spontaneous expression of some feeling was rejected or disapproved of by others that our problems began. As infants, we were too dependent on the care and protection of others to be able to stand up for our right to be individuals. We were not able to absorb too much criticism or disapproval before we began to doubt and mistrust our own feelings.

The cumulative effect is for us to begin to lose touch with our intuitive 'inner selves', and to look outside ourselves more and more for an acceptable way of being as an insurance against the pain of rejection. Here is a simple example. A child is playing in the garden and falls off the swing. The child is hurt, shaken, scared, and a little shocked and, inevitably, starts to cry. Mother hears the cries and runs to respond to them, also a little afraid that the child might be badly hurt. The mother is happy to see there is no real damage, and with a sense of relief she tries to comfort the child. She says, 'It's OK, it doesn't hurt, you're not hurt, be a big boy now, don't cry.' Whilst she does reassure and comfort the child, she also scolds him for making such a fuss, 'Come on now, stop making such a noise or I'll take you indoors and take the swing away.'

Though the mother had the best of intentions, the child learned something in addition to the fact that mother did care. The child discovered that his feelings of hurt, shock and fear were not really recognised or fully understood; in fact they were rejected. In this instance, the mother had not been accepting of the child's feelings. The child did feel comforted, but also began to develop a condition of worth, which, in this example, might have been something like: 'It's not OK to show hurt feelings, being grown-up means to choke back a spontaneous expression of feeling.'

We can learn another lesson from this story. Denial of feelings, or the denial of their expression, is a protection. What may be a *defence* in psychological terms (i.e. the repression, denial or distortion of feelings) may also be a *protection* against the possibility of being denied love or security. The important thing about this behaviour is that it works – it lessens the possibility that love will be withdrawn.

The conditions of worth that we carry from our childhoods into our adult lives often cause problems in our attempts to relate to other adults (and children). Part of the problem is that these conditions of worth are usually hidden, and out of our immediate awareness, but they continue to operate, often in destructive ways.

A Case Study

George was brought up in a household where showing affection through physical contact like hugging, holding hands or kissing was frowned on. George's need to express his feelings in physical ways, to be held or hugged, was continually frustrated. One of his conditions of worth became: 'Physical demonstrations of affection, especially in public places, are always wrong. I risk rejection and disapproval if I behave in this way.' In his later life, George knew *intellectually* that there was nothing really wrong with physical affection, but he found it impossible to touch or be touched without experiencing overwhelming feelings of guilt. Although he was capable of feeling love, he was unable to express or receive it completely, and for all his adult life he has never been able to stay in a relationship with anyone who, quite reasonably, enjoyed and needed physical expressions of warmth.

You can see from this example how conditions of worth can often become ingrained into the structure of families, with one generation passing on its conditions to the next. George's grandparents were just as frosty when it came to touching, and probably their parents were too. However, though it often seems to happen, it is not inevitable that George, if he has children himself, will be the same kind of parent that his parents were in this respect. Children can become very compliant, and accept their conditioning almost without question, but they can also become rebellious and reject their own conditioning. In adult life it is still possible for George to rebel against his own upbringing and to be quite different with his own children.

It is important that we do not run away with the idea that all parental attempts to guide our behaviour end up with unhealthy conditions of worth, or that parents *deliberately* set out to provide problems for us in later life – that would be most unkind, and as a parent myself, I know that is not true. There were obviously some things we needed to learn about life and its hazards from those who cared for us – like not playing in the traffic, for example, or not pouring water on the TV set. The problem for parents is to find ways of guiding and advising, without being over controlling or over protective. Children have a natural curiosity and a desire to explore the fascinating world that surrounds them, and this needs to be nurtured and encouraged.

Conditions of Worth Need Not Be Permanent

The first relationships we experience have a profound effect on the way we conduct the rest of our lives. Our resulting conditions of worth are likely to be complex, and made up of many layers of meaning. Some will be no trouble at all later, others will deeply influence the way we conduct our future relationships on the one hand, and the way we feel about and value ourselves on the other.

As we grow up, our network of relationships expands to include other people: schoolteachers, brothers and sisters, friends and neighbours, aunts and uncles and so on. We learn from these relationships too. Though these learnings may not be as powerful as the first ones, they are significant as some of them will reinforce existing conditions of worth, while other conditions may arise and become incorporated into our sense of self, shaping and refining our personalities.

It is not true that our childhood-acquired conditions of worth need control and limit our behaviour forever. If this were so, there would be no such thing as counselling or psychotherapy. In person centred psychology, it is believed that we can relearn how to be ourselves, and how to free ourselves of destructive or self-defeating behaviour. I discuss counselling and psychotherapy in more detail in Chapter 10; what I want to do now is to stay with more familiar, everyday relationships.

Breaking Free of Conditions

If our conditions of worth are very strong, it can be impossible to break away from them without help. We end up going round in circles, repeating the same old patterns of behaviour, and continually defeating ourselves in our search for a more satisfying way of life. We can help ourselves break this circle by bringing three qualities to our relationships. They are, first, a degree of self-awareness, second the ability to offer empathic and relatively non-judgemental understanding to others, and, third, the ability to communicate both our understanding of others and our own feelings, thoughts and emotions.

Self-awareness concerns how much we know of our early conditioning and how those conditions predict our present day behaviour. For example, if we know that one of our conditions of worth was 'sex is dirty, and wrong', we are at least helped towards some understanding of our present day attitudes towards sex. This is not the end of the story because knowing something to be a fact about ourselves (or at least, a strongly held belief), might help, but it often does not do away with whatever problem is caused by it.

Self-awareness includes being aware of thoughts, emotions and fantasies, as well as abilities, talents, values and so on. It also includes being aware of how behaviour affects others, or how it is interpreted and understood by others. This last point can be quite tricky. People often find it difficult to deal with feedback and reactions about how they are seen and experienced, but getting this kind of feedback is valuable to us all, if we can hear it without getting defensive or feeling criticised.

The Importance of Empathy in Relationships

Empathic understanding and communication are key elements in all successful human relationships. *Empathy* means being able to see the world through the eyes of someone else, stepping into their shoes as it were, and putting aside our own expectations and experiences as far as we can. For adults this can be quite difficult to do at all, and especially so with children; most of us forget how the world looked and felt when we were very young. But empathy is not the same as remembering how things were for us. It involves listening very carefully to the way people speak (and communicate in other ways), and hearing and understanding the feelings and emotions that are being conveyed, as well as the content of what is being spoken about.

You would expect, if empathy was an important quality in relationships, that children of empathic parents would be more likely to grow up well-adjusted, responsible and achieving. You would expect the opposite in children with non-empathic parents, and this is what the research in this area tends to show. For example, Egeland and Stroufe (1981) found that children of 'unavailable' mothers (who were described as emotionally uninvolved and uninterested in their children) found it very difficult to make relationships with others. Pulkkinen (1982) on the other hand, showed that 14-year-old children of parents who were interested in and involved with them were, in general, socially competent, well adjusted and achieved well. By contrast, Pulkkinen also found that children of what were described as 'parent-centred' parents (defined as selfish), were, for example, impulsive, had poor emotional control and were less achieving.

There is a consensus amongst writers from both the person centred school of thought and the psychoanalytic school (most notably, Heinz Kohut, e.g. 1978) that parental empathy is a most important factor in the social development of children. Furthermore, it is thought that non-empathic parents tend to bring up non-empathic children, and it has been shown by Feschbach and Feschbach (1969) that empathic children are likely to be sensitive to the feelings of other children, more able to understand others in conflict situations, and be more cooperative and less aggressive than non-empathic children.

Empathy can, however, be counterproductive if it goes overboard and seems like an unwelcome intrusion—when it is not combined with some sensitivity. Despite this, it is clear from both general research and clinical experience in psychotherapy, that empathy is a powerful factor in determining how far a relationship will be experienced as satisfying to all concerned.

Empathy is not of much use unless it is communicated. You cannot really know if someone is understanding you unless that understanding is shared, checked out, and adjusted if needs be. Within relationships, the degree to which empathic understanding is necessary will vary with the kind of relationship it is. Here, we are concerned with deeper, more intimate relationships which need the people concerned to be understanding of each other, and to learn to appreciate what life is like from the other's point of view.

Empathy is particularly important in parent/child relationships, but when it comes to adult relationships, the presence or absence of empathy and clear communication can be the difference between 'success' and 'failure'. Close relationships, at their best, provide us with the security to be ourselves, without feeling the need to be defensive. They are also where we can explore varying degrees of intimacy, from the warmth of a good friend to the closeness and excitement of a sexual relationship.

It is within our close relationships that conditions of worth get put to the test most. For example, whilst we might desire closeness and intimacy, we might also be afraid of it, or afraid to express intimate thoughts and feelings. Similarly, we almost inevitably will find ourselves relating to our partner in ways that square with early conditioning, yet might actually be experienced as destructive in the present day. One way to illustrate why relationships are so important to us and how they are affected, often very deeply, by past experiences, is with a short case study.

A Second Case Study

Jane and Steven are in their early twenties. They have been together for three years, and recently decided to set up home together. In the last couple of months, what has always been a 'difficult' relationship has taken a turn for the worse. They have started to row constantly, with Steven accusing Jane of being suspicious without good reason, and Jane accusing Steven of being uncaring, inconsiderate and secretive.

Things got bad enough for the two of them to decide to see a counsellor. It felt like a 'make or break' decision, they still had enough love for each other to give things one last try.

Counselling helped them to spend time looking at their relationship in an atmosphere away from the home. They were able to talk about themselves, their feelings for each other, and what went on inside them when the rows started. Jane's childhood had been very difficult. When she was 6-years-old she was adopted, her original parents had split up and disappeared, abandoning her. Her new parents were reasonably good to her, but she had to fit in with a family that already had five older children. She always felt like a bit of a stranger, never really feeling at home with the rest of the family. The new parents had a number of what they called 'golden rules'. One of them Jane remembered particularly well – 'keep your nose out of other people's business.'

Steven was brought up by a professional couple (Steven described them as 'well-off'), who had no other children. He was expected to succeed at school, which he did, and then go to university, which he refused to do. In one counselling session, Steven described how his parents only ever showed approval of him when he succeeded at things they saw as important. They never showed any interest, for example, in Steven's artistic and musical talents. As a result, Steven neglected these talents, and for a time concentrated on 'academic' subjects at school. When he was seventeen, he took up playing the guitar, at which he excelled, and decided to make a career in music. His parents never accepted this decision, and told him, many times, how disappointed they were in him, and how he had 'wasted' his abilities.

In the counselling sessions, a picture gradually emerged of how these two people's conditions of worth were now creating almost insurmountable problems for them. Jane was unable to talk to Steven directly about her thoughts and feelings, and was equally unable to ask him about his. Her condition of worth that revolved around the disapproval of letting others in on your 'business', or taking an interest in theirs prevented this. But she did have a need to know. Her original parents had tried to hide their disagreements from her, and had pretended things were OK when really they were not. She had learned to distrust what she saw and heard, but she was not able to confront things openly. Instead, she resorted to a kind of detective work, picking up clues and half clues, and trying to piece them together herself.

Steven, on the other hand, had learned that things that were important to him were not approved of by others. Though he was not aware of the reason for it, he found it more and more difficult to share his success with Jane. She would find things out about him from friends, or as a result of her 'detective work'.

The relationship they now had could go only one of two ways. Either they could work through these problems, or they could split up. For a time it was touch and go, but gradually they learned to listen to each other anew, to have some empathy for each other, and develop some understanding of how each of them saw the other. Jane learned why Steven seemed secretive, and that to Steven what he was doing was protecting something that had been hurt once before. Steven learned why Jane came across as suspicious, and that to share his successes with her brought them closer together. Because they were now being more understanding of each other and themselves, and were able to communicate more openly with each other, things began to improve.

Their relationship provided opportunities for both Jane and Steven to discover some of their conditions of worth. At first they were unable to move beyond the unconscious repetition of this early conditioning, but with help began to develop new ways of being with each other. The crucial factor was the change in the quality of their communication, which became less defensive and more straightforward. They also learned to listen, first of all to themselves, and then to each other, and as a result, became more understanding and less judgemental of each other.

We can now begin to answer our original question, 'Why are relationships so important?' It is not just because we need others to feel loved by, or to love or work or play with, even though these things can be very satisfying. It is through our relationships that we first of all develop our own unique personality, values, ideas and sense of self. Later, our relationships can help us to discover things about ourselves that we may want to change, as well as things we like and would want to keep the same. The need for people to get together is connected with our need to communicate, to experience ourselves in relation to others, and to get to know selected other people more intimately.

Problems in adult relationships often stem from unhappy experiences in childhood, but being with other people seems such a strong need for most of us, that we would rather put up with all kinds of difficulties than be on or own. Being more self-aware and empathic towards others (and ourselves) makes it more likely that our relationships will be happy ones. Learning how to communicate more openly, and to be less judgemental of others can help us both to get more from our relationships and to contribute more to those we develop throughout life.

Chapter 10
How Do Person Centred Therapists Help?

Ms G.: ... I feel good because ... I somehow feel I'm just beginning to feel those feelings ... I talked about, they're coming out a little bit at a time.

Carl: It's not quite so frightening because you realise, 'Yes, I am able to be in touch with them and they're not overwhelming me, coming out little by little.'

(Long pause)

Ms G.: I somehow wish I could explore more with you.

Carl: You wish?

Ms G.: I wish I could explore more with you because I don't feel frightened with you.

Carl: You feel that this is a fairly safe place, and that I'm a fairly safe person to explore them with.

Ms G.: Yes.

People look for help from counsellors and psychotherapists for many different reasons, most often (though not always) because they are in a personal crisis of some kind. This could be, for example, a bereavement, the ending of a long-term relationship, feelings of overwhelming anxiety, or just plain unhappiness. Other people do not see therapy as the answer to a specific problem, but want to make more sense out of life, or get to know themselves better.

Ms G. does not have a single problem she wants to solve, but feels that her quality of life, and the way she makes relationships is affected by the difficulties she faced as a child. Although she knows something about the circumstances of her childhood, this knowledge alone does not save her from feeling things that trouble her a good deal. The big question for everyone who sees a therapist is, 'How can this person help me?'

Person centred therapy (also referred to as client centred therapy) is based on the principle that human behaviour is motivated by the actualising tendency (the inherent capacity for people to move towards becoming fully functioning). It follows from this that the resources we need to make changes for ourselves already exist within us; they are not supplied from the outside.

One of the best known stories about Carl Rogers concerns the time he was working in Rochester, New York, for the Society for the Prevention of Cruelty to Children. At this time (1928), Rogers saw himself in the psychoanalytic tradition where he expected to make a diagnosis and help children (or parents) gain insights into why they behaved in the way they did. He was working with a mother whose son was very seriously disturbed, but no matter how hard Rogers tried, he could not get the mother to understand the part she had played (according to Rogers) in the emotional disturbance of the boy, and in the end he gave up. The mother asked Rogers if he took parents for therapy, and when Rogers agreed, the mother began to describe all her emotional difficulties concerning her marriage and her low sense of self-esteem. In Rogers' words:

> Real therapy began then, and ultimately it was successful. This incident was one of a number which helped me to experience the fact – only fully realised later – that it is the *client* who knows what hurts, what directions to go, what problems are crucial, what experiences have been deeply buried. It began to occur to me that unless I had a need to demonstrate my own cleverness and learning, I would do better to rely upon the client for the direction of movement in the process (cited in Kirschenbaum and Henderson, 1989a: 13).

This incident, and a number of others like it, were critical in the development of Rogers' approach to counselling and psychotherapy. If he was to help people, then it was not so much a question of diagnosing what was wrong with them and providing appropriate treatment, but more one of *listening* to them and getting a sense of who they were, what troubled them and how they might discover their own resources for putting things right.

Active Listening

All psychotherapists listen to their clients, but Rogers was among the first to notice the therapeutic power of listening and understanding people empathically, and that this form of listening was helpful in its own right. In other words, being fully understood by someone prepared to put their own concerns aside, and concentrate on understanding you and your world helps you understand yourself better and make the changes you need.

Empathy, according to Rogers, means:

> entering into the private perceptual world of the other and becoming

thoroughly at home with it. It involves being sensitive, moment by moment, to the changing felt meanings which flow in this other person, to the fear or rage or tenderness or confusion or whatever that he or she is experiencing... It includes communicating your sensings of the person's world as you look with fresh and unfrightened eyes at elements of which he or she is fearful ... You are a confident companion to the person in his or her inner world (Rogers, 1980: 142).

In the interview with Ms G there are many good examples of empathy, but one of the clearest happens during this exchange:

Ms G.: I, er, I get rid of little bits of it on other people, you know (laughing) you can do something really simple to me and I can resent it, you know and I enjoy feeling resentful.
Carl: You're feeling you let out a little bit of it even though you exaggerate the situation in order to feel that resentment, and it lets out a little of the resentment from the past.
Ms G.: That's exactly it, I didn't use the word 'exaggeration' but, er, situations occur sometimes and I exaggerate them so that they can fit into this pattern so that I can feel the resentment and ... (laughs)
Carl: So you're quite ingenious in finding ways of expressing bits of it.
Ms G.: Yeah, I am ... (long pause) ... (sighs and shakes head).

There are examples of 'deeper empathy' elsewhere in the interview, but this one illustrates the kind of reaction that often happens when a client feels really understood. Rogers used the word 'exaggeration', and it was this that showed Ms G that he had been listening attentively, and understood her very accurately. It seems a simple thing, but in reality it is very hard to do. To stay within a person's experience, and to try and see the world through their eyes (sometimes called their 'frame of reference') is not something we naturally do in our everyday relationships very often. Rogers thought that empathy was so important in counselling that he wrote:

> To my mind, empathy is in itself a healing agent. It is one of the most potent aspects of therapy, because it releases, it confirms, it brings even the most frightened client into the human race. If a person is understood, he or she belongs (Rogers, 1986b).

Empathy is concerned not only with feelings, but with understanding a person's entire frame of reference including feelings, but also including perceptions, thoughts, ideas and meanings. Recent research (e.g. Brodley and Brody, 1990; Merry, 1994) has focused on the way Rogers responded to clients' total perceptions of themselves and the world around them, whether they expressed them in feeling terms or more cognitively. The original way in which Rogers described what he was trying to do as 'reflection of feelings' is, in fact, a little misleading.

As he pointed out, the counsellor's intentions are more complex than making simple reflections:

> I am trying to determine whether my understanding of the client's inner world is correct – whether I am seeing it as he or she is experiencing it at this moment. Each response of mine contains the unspoken question, 'Is this the way it is for you. Am I catching just the colour and texture and flavour of the personal meaning you are experiencing right now? If not, I wish to bring my perception in line with yours (Rogers, 1986a).

When clients feel empathically understood they are enabled to reveal and express more of their 'inner worlds'. We can see this quite clearly with Ms G. throughout the interview. Paradoxically, however, it is not the therapist's intention to produce this effect, even though this is what often happens. The therapist sets out to do one thing only, and that is to understand his or her client as deeply as possible.

Two More 'Core Conditions' of Person Centred Psychotherapy

Being empathic is not, however, the whole story. Rogers thought there were two more attitudes or 'ways of being' as he put it, which, when combined with empathy, produced the 'core conditions' of effective therapy. These he called *congruence* (or genuineness, or authenticity), and *unconditional positive regard* (or warmth or prizing). Congruence means that therapists need to know themselves well, be non-defensive in their relationships with clients, and prepared to show themselves for who they are, rather than adopt an objective, uninvolved or distant attitude. They need to be aware of their own internal processes, moods, thoughts and feelings, but this does not mean that they should express every thought, feeling or mood as the therapy progresses. Therapists need to be sure enough of themselves to know when and how to express their feelings to their clients, and to do so in ways that respect and are not judgemental of them.

Unconditional positive regard is similar to the attitude of good parents who prize and value their children, no matter what they do. Even though they might object to some behaviour, this does not extend to being dismissive of or condemning the child as a person. The therapist maintains the attitude that, no matter how awful some of their clients' behaviour may have been, they are, nevertheless, human beings struggling to grow, change and develop in positive, social and constructive directions.

Rogers' idea, that it is these three attitudes that are all important, was arrived at after a period of painstaking investigation into what seemed to help clients and what did not. In the 1940s, together with his colleagues, Rogers made hours of recordings of counsellors and their clients, a technically very difficult and cumbersome operation in those days. From these recordings they tried to identify what it was that helped clients explore their lives more fully, and what it was that hindered them. Remarkably, it was not the technical expertise, or how learned therapists were in theories of psychology and personal change that counted. It was the way the therapist related to the client, the kind of relationship that was established, that made the difference. From these investigations Rogers first formed his hypothesis that it was the quality of the relationship and certain attitudes of the therapist that were both *necessary and sufficient* to help clients make changes (Rogers, 1957a).

Mearns and Thorne (1988) have stressed this last point very strongly:

> Research suggests that experienced counsellors of different traditions are in broad agreement on the fact that the *relationship* between client and counsellor is of fundamental importance in counselling (for example Fiedler, 1950). The distinctive feature about the person-centred approach is that it does not just pay lip service to the importance of the relationship, but actually takes that as the aim of the counselling process with *every* client. In the person-centred approach there is no withdrawal from the relationship and retreat into exercises, interpretation or analysis of the client's behaviour. The relationship is *all*-important: if that is healthy then the counselling outcome has the best chance of being productive (p. 21).

When Rogers published his work, the words 'necessary and sufficient' were met with scepticism and disbelief by counsellors and psychotherapists. Rogers was proposing something revolutionary that went against everything that had been taken as true up to that point. The conventional wisdom was that success depended on an expert, accurate diagnosis which is (in psychoanalytic terms at least) to be followed by interpretations of the client's unconscious motives for his or her behaviour. Rogers offered an alternative way that trusted the actualising tendency of each client to become active within a relationship with specific qualities. Clients were understood and approached as able to find solutions to their own problems. The power of the expert, so familiar within the 'medical model' of illness was diminished, and a more egalitarian or equal relationship was put in its place.

How Emotional Disturbance Is Created

The cause of emotional disturbance is, according to person centred theory, damage to the capacity of the actualising tendency to guide behaviour. This damage is created by being treated as only of conditional value, or no value at all, by significant people in childhood. The child who experiences a lack of positive regard (or its complete absence) from parents and others, is likely to end up with little or no self-esteem and with a negative self-image. This is what makes the non-judgemental, unconditionally accepting attitude so important. These days, person centred therapists are beginning to think about empathy and congruence as the 'ways of being' which enable them to experience unconditional positive regard for their clients (Bozarth, 1993). According to Bozarth, unconditional positive regard is the most potent agent of change, releasing the client's actualising tendency and capacity for self-healing.

Mearns and Thorne (1988) have offered a straightforward way of understanding how person centred psychology explains the creation of psychological disturbance:

1. At the beginning of life, person and organismic self are one.
2. Organismic self meets hostility, disapproval, rejection or other negative feelings. The person becomes confused and anxious because the need for positive regard is paramount.
3. A self-concept is formed which is conditioned by the responses experienced by the organismic self and which at the same time seeks to protect the person from future disapproval or hostility. Self-concept and organismic self are often in conflict but maintain an uneasy communication.
4. Continuing negativity is encountered and the self-concept is further adjusted in the light of this. The need to avoid yet more disapproval is strengthened. Within the person the voice of the organismic self becomes fainter.
5. The self-concept is reinforced and becomes increasingly divorced from the organismic self which eventually falls silent. The person is now locked into a self-concept which is usually poor and always out of touch with the organismic self. He or she is disturbed (p. 13).

The therapeutic relationship acts as a kind of re-education for the client. He or she is increasingly able to emerge from behind defensive barriers, and to acknowledge experiences with more freedom. There is no need to deny or distort experiences and feelings because there is no threat of positive regard being withdrawn. When Ms G. says, *'I wish I could explore more with you, because I don't feel frightened with you'*, it is safe to assume that she is beginning to feel more free to express herself because she perceives no threat in the relationship.

The combination of the three core conditions provides this non-threatening atmosphere. Conditions of worth, defences, denials and distortions can now be re-evaluated from an adult perspective, and the person can move closer to trusting her internal valuing process. This represents a shift in the 'locus of evaluation' away from dependence on the evaluations of others for our feelings of self-regard and self-esteem (an external locus of evaluation), towards an internal locus of evaluation in which we are able to trust and value our own experiences and feelings about ourselves.

This makes it possible to respond to our original question, 'How do person centred therapists help?' by reference not to what is done in terms of techniques or treatment plans, but in terms first of the therapist's way of being with clients, and second in terms of the client's own psychological resources. This is a typically humanistic way of thinking about the process. In other words, clients are viewed as capable and resourceful, with the power to make changes for themselves. Person centred therapy is not a matter of *doing* something *to* people, more a matter of *being with* them in particular ways.

The Skills of the Therapist

This does not mean that there are no skills involved, or that there is no real discipline. Skills are the specific ways in which therapists put their values and attitudes into practice through their behaviour with their clients (Merry and Lusty, 1993). The skills are really those of good listening and clear communication. The therapist tries to sense the emotional meanings contained within the client's words, and tries to communicate to the client the extent to which he or she understands. Carl Rogers never tried to interpret what might be the 'real' meaning behind the words, only to understand more accurately what the client was able, at that time, to express. He consistently took the attitude that the client was the only real 'expert'. If he could meet with this person in a non-judgemental and understanding way, more complex layers of meaning and feeling would gradually emerge into awareness, at the client's own pace and in his or her own way.

Although there are some similarities between person centred therapy and some other approaches, only person centred therapy sees the relationship itself as the catalyst for change. This is still a controversial position within the therapy world generally, but a good deal of Rogers' work is now incorporated into other theories. Most agree that the personal qualities brought to relationships with clients are very significant in determining whether or not therapy will be successful.

In the transcript of Ms G.'s interview, you can see that she was able to talk about things in a new way for her. Perhaps even more importantly, she was able to re-experience some of her past emotions in an atmosphere of care and trust. It is as if, in feeling more and more deeply understood without being judged, Ms G. was able to revisit her childhood and experience the feelings of powerlessness she had as a 4-year-old. She was able to see how the anger and resentment built up, and how she tried to keep it hidden from herself and others. But, as she says, little bits of anger or resentment would come out quite unexpectedly, and she would find herself reacting as an adult in ways that were influenced and shaped by those past experiences.

A Way of Being

Carl Rogers referred to his approach as a 'way of being', rather than a 'way of doing'. In other words he thought that change resulted from a client's experience of being heard, cared for and understood, not as a result of special techniques designed to stimulate particular feelings or emotions. He had a number of ways of describing his approach to human growth and development, but perhaps few as eloquent as this:

> I have described therapeutic development as a 'self-initiated process of learning to be free'. This learning is composed of movement from, as well as movement toward. Clients move away from being driven by inner forces they do not understand, away from fear and distrust of these deep feelings and of themselves, and away from living by values they have taken from others. They move toward acceptance and enjoyment of their own feelings, toward valuing and trusting the deeper layers of their nature, finding strength in their own uniqueness, and living by values based in their own experience. This learning, this movement, enables them to live as more individuated, more creative, more responsive and more responsible persons. Clients are often sharply aware of such directions in themselves, even as they move with apprehension toward being freely themselves (Rogers, cited in Kirschenbaum and Henderson, 1989b: 83).

Some Criticisms of Person Centred Therapy

Criticisms of person-centred therapy fall into three categories: (1) Rogers' view of human nature is naive and simplistic, (2) the reliance on the quality of the relationship is unjustified, and (3) the research does not support the notion that the core conditions are both necessary and *sufficient*.

Human Nature

Most criticism of Rogers' view of human nature is based on the mistaken impression that Rogers thought human beings to be 'basically good'. It is much more accurate to say that 'humans are growth oriented and will naturally progress towards the fulfilment of their innate potential if psychological conditions are favourable' (Thorne, 1992: 66).

Criticism from the Freudian school of thought tends to concentrate on the idea that Rogers did not take enough account of the forces of the unconscious. Freud was pessimistic about human nature, and believed the unconscious to contain powerfully destructive forces, but, as we have seen, Rogers held a distinctly different, more optimistic view.

The Relationship

An important critic of Rogers, Van Belle (1980), argues that a therapeutic relationship of the kind Rogers advocated might produce a sense of dependency on the therapist, rather than the discovery of personal resources and autonomy. A second common criticism is that simply supplying the 'core conditions' is not enough to promote change and development. This criticism is the source of much debate and is not easily resolved by reference to the research literature (see the discussion below).

A third source of criticism comes from the psychoanalysts. Many are sceptical of Rogers' claim that transference (the unconscious repetition of past feelings and behaviour in the present) should not be treated differently from any other phenomenon that arises within the client/therapist relationship. Rogers, however, did not alter his position on transference, which he outlined in 1951:

> ... if the definition being used is the transfer of infantile attitudes to a present relationship in which they are inappropriate, then very little, if any, transference is present ... In client-centred therapy, however, this involved and persistent dependent transference relationship does not tend to develop (Rogers, 1951: 199).

Rogers was quite hostile to the idea of transference occupying a central theoretical and practical position in psychotherapy and wrote strongly about it:

> To deal with transference feelings as a very special part of therapy, making their handling the very core of therapy, is to my mind a grave mistake. Such an approach fosters dependence and lengthens therapy. It creates a whole new problem, the only purpose of which appears to be the intellectual satisfaction of the therapist – showing the elaborateness of his or her expertise. I deplore it (Rogers, 1987: 183–4).

The Research

The problem with the research into the effectiveness of person centred psychotherapy is that little of it has adequately tested Rogers' original hypothesis. Significantly, this hypothesis included the client's *perception* of the relationship, and where studies have incorporated this they have not included all of the hypothesised core conditions operating in a unified way. Even so, research has indicated that the presence of the core conditions is positively related to successful outcomes. Patterson (1984) thinks that much of the research *does* indicate support for the necessity, if not the sufficiency, of the core conditions, but researchers themselves do not report or discuss their own results accurately.

A review of the research literature on the effectiveness of therapy was carried out by Smith et al. (1980). They found that it was effective in helping people, but could find no reliable evidence that any one method was any more effective than any other.

Rogers and Dymond (1954), from a person centred perspective, explored different aspects of change in clients' self-concept during and after therapy. They used the 'Q-sort' method in which clients rank order a series of statements that describe 'how I see myself now', and 'how I would most like to be'. They found that changes in self-perception were clearly related to positive outcomes in therapy. Rogers et al. (1967) also tried to test the effectiveness of person centred therapy among hospitalised schizophrenics. Although the results were inconclusive, this research led Rogers and his colleagues to reinforce the importance of 'congruence' as a core condition.

McLeod (1993: 183) thinks that Rogers and his associates made significant contributions to the research for four reasons: (1) they showed that the processes of counselling and psychotherapy are not 'mysterious or elusive', but can be the subject of proper research, (2) their research represents probably the most successful attempt to test counselling theory and evolve new concepts, (3) they showed that research could be fruitfully integrated with practice, and (4) they showed it was possible to explore the experiences and perceptions of clients undergoing counselling.

My Own Position

I think that Rogers' positive and creative contributions to our understanding of the process far outweigh the doubts and criticisms summarised above. This does not mean that I believe Rogers' theory to be complete or without some contradictions and weaknesses. For example, you can read Rogers' description of the qualities of effective therapists (high levels of empathy, congruence and positive regard) as standards that would be difficult, if not impossible, to maintain consistently with every client. It can be difficult to hold on to Rogers' idea that these qualities are to be worked towards, rather than attained once and for all. In practice it can be very challenging to sustain unconditional positive regard when a client is describing behaviour that I would find unacceptable in myself.

I have also sometimes wondered about the usefulness of the term 'a way of being'. I find it an attractive concept, and it captures very succinctly Rogers' notion that it is our 'humanness' that we bring to others in distress, rather than techniques or systems. On the other hand, Rogers was a very skilled communicator, and sharing his empathy and understanding seemed to come naturally to him. By contrast, I have sometimes found myself lost for words, or searching for ways to communicate my thoughts and feelings that can be easily heard and understood by my clients. Rogers avoided talking about 'skills', but I have found it essential to spend time working on my own abilities to say clearly what I mean.

When I refer to my own experience, both as a client and as a practitioner, I am very optimistic. I have seen and shared in some slow and steady progress and some dramatic shifts of perception and self-esteem. I appreciate the way person centred therapy respects the needs of each person, and is willing to travel alongside each person in his or her journey towards self-discovery, without trying to impose any particular view of what a person *should* be.

Section III
Learning and Growing

One of the most important institutions with which we all have some contact is education. From playgroup to university, the quality of our experience of education has a profound effect on the attitudes we take to learning. Since you are reading this book, it is most probably safe to assume that your education was (and perhaps still is) successful. For many people, successful education means being able to read, to do at least some mathematics, to be able to think in certain ways, to be able to solve problems and to be familiar with information and ideas. We should also keep in mind that education is not something that happens to us only in schools and other similar institutions. Even though the examples and case-studies in the following chapters are from schools and colleges, learning and growing is, or can be, a life-long activity.

It is understandable that the majority of people would say that education is about learning facts and how to make some sense out of them. Fewer people, however, would say that feelings and emotions have much part to play in the educational process, and fewer still would explicitly make room for including emotions in the teaching and learning process. But how we feel about our experiences at school and college has a significant effect on the extent to which we can make use of the educational opportunities offered to us. As you might expect, the very early experiences we have of education affect, either in positive or negative ways, our attitudes towards learning from then on.

The current political attitude towards education in the UK is concerned with standardisation, testing and the acquisition of facts and skills useful in later life. I certainly do not deny the importance of being 'well educated' or skilled, but it does seem to me that the move towards more so-called 'traditional values' in education is in danger of making the classroom a more remote and less completely human place. Being educated is part and parcel of the experience of growing towards maturity, and maturity involves a lot more than the intellectual or cognitive side of life.

One thing, however, must not be forgotten. It is the collective voice of those hundreds, perhaps thousands of teachers and educators who, over the years as well as in the present day, have argued for child centred, humanistic values. Carl Rogers is part of this tradition from an American perspective, but 'progressive' ideas in education have a tradition in the UK and Europe that goes back several hundred years. Rousseau (1712–1778), for example, is frequently given credit for being the inspiration of most of the more progressive ideas we now see in modern education:

> He was perhaps the first and greatest exponent of a truly child-centred education, based on a belief in the innate goodness of children, and all later efforts to reformulate an education related to the psychology of childhood owe him a debt (Lawrence, 1970).

Others, such as Pestalozzi (1746–1827), were greatly influenced by Rousseau and shared with him a belief in the positive, creative characteristics of humankind. Pestalozzi's faith in love as the vital force in education permeated his entire approach. Lack of love, he believed, was the cause of 'backwardness' and 'delinquency'. The aim of education for Pestalozzi was the development of the whole person, the creative powers, intellect and feelings of each individual. Pestalozzi was a teacher who experimented with his theories and inspired educators to think seriously of the child as the centre of education. From his time on, the way was open for teachers to find ways of making schools more responsive to the needs and development of children.

The early part of the twentieth century saw a further influential development in progressive educational ideas – the 'Montessori Method'. Montessori's view was that children should be given the freedom to explore the world in their own ways and to become independent of the teacher. She hated the idea of

> children, like butterflies mounted on pins, are fastened each to his place, the desk, spreading the useless wings of barren and meaningless knowledge which they have acquired (Montessori, 1912).

In the USA, John Dewey (1859–1952) also argued for more child centred values. One of his criticisms was that education

> had its centre of gravity outside the child ... in the teacher, the textbook, anywhere and everywhere you please except in the immediate instincts and activities of the child himself (Garforth, 1966).

Dewey thought that the immediate problem for educators lay in finding what conditions must necessarily be fulfilled in order that study and learning could take place naturally. He shared the view that children could be trusted to learn and grow naturally:

> The primary root of all educative activity is in the instinctive, impulsive

attitudes and activities of the child, and not in the presentation and application of external material (Dewey, 1906).

Dewey also believed that the reason why so much educational practice lags far behind theory is that few teachers have themselves experienced the kind of education in which many of them theoretically believe. He wanted changes in the way schools organise materials and methods of instruction so that information is not divorced from action. One of his most significant remarks, and one with which Carl Rogers would have had a great deal of sympathy, was:

> One thing that 'Nature' may be said to utter is that there are conditions of educational efficiency, and that till we have learned what these conditions are and have learned to make our practices accord with them, the noblest and most ideal of our aims are doomed to suffer (Dewey, 1915).

Rogers' views on education have had some impact on both sides of the Atlantic, notably after the publication of his first book on education, *Freedom to Learn* (Rogers, 1969, now out of print) in the 1960s and its revised and updated version, *Freedom to Learn for the Eighties* (Rogers, 1983). It is true to say, however, that this impact has not been extensive in influencing the ways in which modern schools organise their business. Rogers thought that classrooms should be places where the emotional and intellectual lives of children and young adults should be given equal value. He saw the capacity for people to learn intellectually and grow and develop emotionally as being woven together so that they become inseparable. The many teachers and educational theorists who share these views today might be encouraged by the examples that follow, in this section, of people for whom the concept of a child centred education is still very much alive.

Rogers' experience of people in the counselling room led him to believe that the individual's capacity for change, growth and development was almost unlimited. As we have seen in the previous section, the relationships people form with each other have profound effects on their personal and interpersonal functioning. Young children are particularly vulnerable to negative or hurtful attitudes towards them, and particularly open to growth through positive and creative relationships with significant others. For most children, some form of schooling is their first experience of being in the company of many others, both children and adults.

It is not only attitudes and behaviour towards individual learners by individual teachers that are important. Person centred education is about the organisation of the classroom, and the school or college as a whole, and this is as much a question of the politics of education as it is a question of educational or psychological theory. The chapters that follow are, in the main, derived from the experiences of teachers or, in one case, a child counsellor currently working in education. They illustrate both the political issues of how schools should be organised, and the psychological questions concerning how children should be treated within them.

By way of introduction to the following chapters, it is worth summarising how Carl Rogers viewed conventional education, and in what directions he thought changes needed to be made.

In Rogers' view, conventional education has the following characteristics:

- The teacher is the possessor of knowledge, the student the expected recipient. In other words, there is a huge gulf in status between the teacher and the learner.
- The lecture, the textbook, or some other means of verbal intellectual instruction are the major methods of getting knowledge into the recipient. The examination measures the extent to which the student has received it. These are the central elements of this kind of education.
- The teacher is the possessor of power, the student the one who obeys.
- Rule by authority is the accepted policy in the classroom.
- Trust is at a minimum.
- The subjects (students) are best governed by being kept in an intermittent or constant state of fear.
- Democracy and its values are ignored and scorned in practice.
- There is no place for the whole person in the educational system, only for her intellect (Rogers, 1983: 185–7).

On the other hand, the person centred approach is radically different. Provided the leadership of the school is trusting of the capacities of people to think for themselves and to learn in different kinds of ways, some or all of the following characteristics become possible:

- The facilitative teacher shares with others – students, and possibly also parents or community members – the responsibility for the learning process.
- The facilitator provides learning resources, from within herself and her own experience, from books or materials or community resources.
- The student develops her own programme of learning, alone or in cooperation with others.
- A facilitative learning climate is provided.
- The focus is primarily on fostering the continuing process of learning.
- The discipline necessary to reach the student's goals is a self-discipline.

- The evaluation of the extent and significance of the student's learning is made primarily by the learner.
- In this growth-promoting climate, the learning tends to be deeper, proceeds at a more rapid rate, and is more pervasive in the life and behaviour of the student than is learning acquired in the traditional classroom (Rogers, 1983: 188–9).

I do not expect a book such as this to provide a comprehensive exploration of each of these characteristics. I do invite you, however, on reading the chapters that follow, to consider how far the humanistic ideas discussed in them make sense to you.

Chapter 11
Can Person Centred Values Be 'Lived' in Classrooms?

Education is a process involving much more than just intellectual or cognitive activity. This chapter describes the values and characteristics of child centred education, in particular the qualities of person centred teachers. I also discuss, briefly, some of the research that has been done to determine how far the interpersonal qualities of teachers affect learning, and I give some examples of how early experiences in the classroom affected the education of individual people, now adults.

Person centred psychology views learning as a life-long and natural process involving curiosity, exploration and experimentation. This is not such an unusual attitude, and has occurred many times throughout the history of organised education. In the introduction to this section I mentioned the ideas of John Dewey, and Pestalozzi who believed that it was lack of love that led to 'backwardness' and 'delinquency'. In the nineteenth century, Montessori wanted to give children the freedom to explore the world in their own way, independently of the teacher. These views were shared by A.S. Neil, creator of Summerhill, a 'free' school, in 1921:

> When my wife and I began, we had one main idea ... to make the school fit the child instead of making the child fit the school (Neil, 1937).

Later, Neil went further, and remarked that children do not need teaching as much as they need love and understanding, but he was careful to describe the love he meant as being not of the sentimental, possessive kind. To Neil love meant, 'being on the side of the child', so that the child felt love and approval (Neil, 1926).

The Whole Person in the Classroom

The thing that all these educators (and many others) have in common is a determination to include the whole person of the child in the educational process. This involves valuing feelings as much as thoughts, and recognising that these two sides of a person mutually affect each other. Carl Rogers' hypothesis was that people are able to be less

defensive and more open to new 'ways of being' whenever they experience a relationship based on empathy, realness (or congruence) and
unconditional positive regard. We go into this concept in full in other
chapters, but, briefly, empathy is the ability to see the world as others
see it; congruence is being genuine and open rather than playing a
role; and unconditional positive regard is having a caring, non-judgemental attitude. The relationship between learner and teacher plays a
significant part in how well the learner is able to use the educational
opportunities available in school or lecture room. What Rogers had
learned about the way people change in therapy, he thought might
apply to people in other contexts, and particularly so in education
where people are in the process of many changes, not only in their
skills and knowledge, but also in attitudes, values and self-concept.

The values of traditional school and college education, are, as
Rogers observed, reflections of the values of the wider social and political context in which schools and colleges exist. For example, school
students are not generally trusted to be self-directing and self-motivat-
ing, but rather are treated as relatively passive recipients of knowledge,
kept under control by authoritarian traditions. In other words, many
schools display very little trust in people and their potentials. To trust
people more would be to loosen the controls over them and to rely
more on the individual's tendency towards constructive change and
creativity.

The Relationship Between Teacher and Learner

A most important issue here is the quality of the relationships that
become established between those doing the learning and those doing
the teaching. If these relationships are characterised by distrust, negative judgementalism and a lack of understanding, then learners are
unlikely to feel safe enough to take the risks that are often involved in
the process of change. Learners will be unwilling to disclose their feelings of insecurity or inadequacy, or lack of intellectual understanding if
they feel they will be negatively judged for having them. If they do not
feel acceptable as individual people in the classroom, their capacities to
learn will be stifled, and learning will become associated with fear of
failure rather than with the excitement of discovery so evident in very
young children.

There are many complex factors involved in how the educational
process is experienced by children and students. Some are connected
with the way in which the institution is organised in terms of the distribution and exercise of power and authority. An institution that operates from the point of view that learners need to be controlled and
subject to strict externally imposed disciplinary codes will be experienced in ways that are different from a school that values freedom of

choice, self-expression and self-discipline. However, whatever kind of institution it is, and whatever kind of values it operates, individual learners will experience it largely through the contact they have with other individuals including friends but, most significantly, the teachers.

Person centred psychology views the relationships that develop between teachers and learners as very important, and two major pieces of research have provided some significant findings in this regard. It has been found that students tend to learn more, and behave more constructively in the classroom when teachers show good understanding of their students as people, when they show they care for them, and when they are genuine. In the USA, the National Consortium for Humanizing Education (NCHE) conducted a lengthy and complex research study to determine how far teachers high and low in these 'facilitative conditions' affected their students' capacity to learn. Without going into too much detail here (the work is discussed extensively in Rogers, 1983), these researchers found that in classrooms where teachers showed empathy, congruence and respect for their students, the students showed enhanced problem-solving skills, asked more questions, were more involved in their learning, had higher levels of cognition and showed greater levels of creativity, for example, than in classrooms with teachers low in these qualities.

In another part of the study it was found that 'educationally handicapped' students with teachers high in empathy, congruence and positive regard missed fewer days of school during the year, maintained or increased their scores on self-concept measures, maintained or increased their scores in IQ tests and made greater gains on academic achievement measures than similar students with teachers low in these qualities. The researchers came to the conclusion that, 'for students identified as having learning difficulties, the teacher's level of interpersonal facilitation was the single most important contributor to the amount of gain on all outcome measures' (Roebuck et al., 1976, cited in Rogers, 1983: 207).

Research results from the USA are often treated with some scepticism in Europe because of the differences in educational traditions and organisation of state schooling. In Germany, however, two German researchers decided to test the American results by conducting similar research in their own schools. Again, this research is discussed extensively in Rogers (1983) but, in summary, the researchers found:

> In all of the school studies, empathic understanding, genuineness, warm respect, and nondirective activities proved to significantly facilitate the quality of pupils' intellectual contributions during the lesson, their spontaneity, their independence and initiative, their positive feelings during the lesson, and their positive perception of the teacher. Teachers who were rated high on all four dimensions felt more content with themselves and their lessons. Furthermore, all the studies indicated that low ratings on understanding,

genuineness, respect and nondirective facilitation and high ratings on directive leading accompanied lower levels of pupil intellectual performance and significantly negative emotional experiences (Tausch and Tausch, cited in Rogers, 1983: 217).

There are strong indications that the positive effects of teachers high in the facilitative conditions are not dependent on particular cultural or organisational circumstances. Teachers with high levels of the values, attitudes and interpersonal skills I have described tend to encourage more learning than teachers low in those attitudes and personal qualities. How vulnerable children can be to unhappy relationships with teachers, and how encouraged they can be by positive ones, are illustrated by the experiences that follow.

Two Case Studies

Catherine is now 28 years old and has recently been awarded a diploma by a polytechnic (now a university). Her course was in textiles and design. Her 'story' is given, more or less, in her own words.

> My earliest memory of school days is when I was about 7- or 8-years-old. I remember sitting in what seemed like a huge hall, surrounded by more kids than I can ever remember seeing in one place before. The teacher was a man, he seemed huge to me. We were told to make up a story, a kind of comic strip composed of our own words, pictures cut from magazines and our own drawings. My story was about my pet white mouse called Sandy who I had found dead in his cage a few days earlier. I remember being really upset finding his little body all still and stiff that morning. When we had finished, we had to show our work to the class and talk about it in front of them. I was terrified, I had never done anything like this before, and I was absolutely tongue-tied. Somehow, when it came to my turn, I managed to stutter out a few sentences, but it was almost impossible to say anything sensible. When I got to the picture I had drawn of Sandy lying dead in his cage, I started to cry. The teacher said, 'What a lot of fuss about a dead rat'. I was absolutely mortified, especially when the other kids started laughing. I think he must have realised how thoughtless and hurtful he had been because he tried to console me, but it was too late. I hated school from that day on, I wouldn't speak to any of the teachers, and I think they began to think of me as stupid or backward. I never did well at school, and I left as soon as I could. It wasn't until I was in my twenties that I began to regret having no real education and I went to evening classes. Much to everyone's surprise (but not my own) I did rather well. I'm glad I made it in the end, but I really resent all the time wasted, and when I think about that teacher I can still feel the pain and humiliation he caused me.

This second account is from a man, James, now in his thirties. He had a very unhappy home life as his father was in prison for most of James' childhood. James had been in children's homes several times, and foster homes twice, each time separated from his two younger sisters.

I don't remember much about my primary school days, other than they were disrupted a lot. I think I had been to about six different schools by the time I was 11-years-old. For me, the turning point came when I was fourteen at secondary school. It was a big, bustling inner city school in a pretty down and out area in North London. I was just about hopeless at most subjects except English. I was in a gang at that age, and we were responsible for most of the trouble in the school. I got suspended twice, once when I was caught shoplifting. My English teacher was a woman in her mid-thirties. The thing about her that marked her out for me from all the other teachers (though I have to say most were pretty decent) was that she listened and took an interest. She used to spend time with me and a couple of the others, and she encouraged us to join the drama club that had become more or less inactive. About five of us wrote a futuristic play about a gang of inter-planetary vandals whose aim was to start a new religion based on the graffiti recently discovered in twentieth century underground stations. We put everything we had into that play, using stories and incidents that had really happened to us. The teacher, Mrs B., really encouraged us. She would get us to tell stories from our own lives, and then exaggerate and dramatise them. She was interested in the way we felt about things and about ourselves. She is the only person I ever spoke to at any length about my father being in prison. She let us devise our own way of putting the result on the stage, which we did at the end of the year. Up until that point, I had been thought of as 'thick', but we wrote some good stuff. Since then I've had a play produced professionally, had four short stories published, and been on the radio. When I think about Mrs B. I always offer up a silent prayer. She never labelled me as stupid, even though I used to play stupid a lot. I really got into reading and writing in a big way at school, but it was down to Mrs B.'s approach to us which was, 'You can do it'. If she had written me off like most of the other teachers did, I dread to think where I would've ended up. In prison like my father, probably.

There are many stories such as these, and if you recall your own school days you will probably recollect similar situations. The research described briefly above supports the idea that relationships with teachers (and others) can have profoundly damaging or creative outcomes as far as individual school experiences are concerned. The next chapter develops this theme a little more, giving the example of how one child, generally labelled as 'difficult' was encountered by a counsellor trained in the PCA.

Chapter 12
Who Will Listen to the Children?

Schools and their individual classrooms are busy, often noisy places. Every day, schools have to respond to the needs of many people, and they need to evolve means of keeping order so that they do not become chaotic and bewildering places. A classroom of, say, thirty children can easily be disrupted by behaviour that undermines the structure and organisation on which teaching and learning depend. The hurt, angry or violent child can become so disruptive that it seems impossible to allow him or her to continue because other children become affected by behaviour that is not consistent with the maintenance of order and organisation. Yet there are many hurt and angry children. Some become withdrawn and uncommunicative, others act out their hurt and anger, and all give cause for concern in their different ways.

One answer is to remove highly disruptive children from ordinary schools, and place them in special units where their behaviour can more easily be controlled. For some children, such a move can be highly beneficial, but for others it confirms them as failures and labels them as 'no-hopers'. Another way is to try and work with the child within the school; to provide that child with an experience that shows he or she is still valued as a person, even though some behaviour cannot be accepted in the classroom. What follows is a brief case study involving a counsellor working in a school, and the hurt and angry feelings of a young child, Marie.

A Case Study – Marie

Jeannette Weaver works with the Urban Learning Foundation in East London. She is trained in the Person Centred Approach to counselling, and believes that children should be heard and understood in as non-judgemental and accepting way as possible. Jeannette works with individual children in schools, sometimes in the classroom alongside other children, sometimes with children on their own. This is her story, in her words, about Marie.

I first knew Marie only by reputation. She was always outside the head-teacher's office, or standing somewhere in the playground where she'd been put because of something she'd done; but I had my first real encounter with her when she was brought into a classroom where I was working, because she was being so difficult in her own class.

I don't think I've ever seen a child so physically angry. She was just exploding all over the place; she was out of control. There was no sense at all that she really knew what she was doing; she was just hell bent on destruction, wanting to make as much noise and create as much chaos as she could. She was throwing tables and chairs, and I had to restrain her from running out of the classroom, just by leaning against the door with my arms round her and holding her until she stopped. I still remember the look on her face; she looked very intense – locked in.

A couple of months later, I was asked to work with her as her counsel-lor. I suppose I was expecting to meet a bolshy, hard, cold, uncommunica-tive, resistant person – but she absolutely wasn't any of those things. In fact, I was just delighted to see what this child was like, and from day one she was incredibly rewarding to work with.

She was with a teacher who was finding Marie very difficult, so it was to give the teacher a break, as much as anything, that it was decided I should withdraw her from the classroom. From the beginning I saw her twice a week. She was very forthcoming, very open; she found it very easy to talk about being angry, and incredibly easy to talk about the injustice she suf-fered; she felt strongly that she was judged before anybody knew what she had done – and that was absolutely what it was like in school. You only had to mention her name and almost everyone declared her guilty.

So we talked about her angry feelings and we made a lovely book. About half of it was about her anger; she drew pictures of things that made her angry, and what she looked like when she was angry; and then you turned the book over, and it was about happy feelings, things that made her happy, what she looked like when she was happy. She wrote, too; it took a long time to make the book, and eventually she took it back into the class. She presented it to the class, and it was left there.

So it was a funny situation. I had quickly and easily formed a relation-ship with this incredibly sensitive, soft, caring child – but all I was hearing from adults and children was, 'Oh, Marie ... no need to say any more ...'

Pretty quickly after the beginning of the next school year, there was pres-sure to have Marie moved to a special unit. Her teacher was very angry her-self at the time, and found it difficult to handle Marie's anger as well. I was disgusted; in my view the kind of move being considered would do Marie far more harm than good, and would lead to her being labelled a 'no-hoper'. What she needed was to be taken seriously, accepted as she was, acknowledged as a very angry person, and supported and accommodated in the school.

The thought of Marie being moved made me furious, and I told certain people so. I think my anger took them by surprise. I think they thought of me as a soft and gentle person, but when I spoke they knew I meant it. I suppose I was Marie's voice, because no one would ever have listened to her. It was like Marie saying, 'Can't you see? That isn't what I need, this is what I need.' It was a real passion – uncompromising. I was completely, totally clear that she did need to stay in school, and she didn't need to be cast out. I am not saying she wouldn't have benefited from being at the special centre, but I just knew that the most important thing was that she wasn't got rid of, that she was accepted, and that, in the end, is what happened.

'I just kept being very positive about Marie whenever she was mentioned, and quite quickly people were saying that they didn't hear her name being mentioned so much, and she wasn't in the playground book so much, and she wasn't outside the Head's room so much. Now, she's with a very experienced teacher who's been very understanding of her, and she's stayed in the school. She's been held.

When I first knew Marie, she was totally powerless. I don't think she could have been more powerless because she was prejudged. Her name came first, and as soon as her name was seen, that was it; she never came into the picture. But now the change is quite unbelievable. People actually see Marie. They see that she is a wonderful, rich person who gets very angry sometimes.'(Weaver, 1991.)

What lessons can we learn from this story? First, Jeannette's way of working with Marie was concerned with acknowledging the whole person of Marie, not just the angry part. Jeannette wanted to see Marie and to encounter her, as she said, 'as a rich person who gets very angry sometimes', not simply as a disruptive or difficult child. We can conceptualise this as an example of Jeannette's unconditional positive regard. Second, Jeannette's concern was with listening to the child and, through this, to try and understand the world from the child's point of view. Put another way, Jeannette tried to enter Marie's frame of reference and to understand its complexities – in short, to empathise with her. Third, it is probable that Jeannette was a very real person to Marie; someone who did not label her or judge her, but was willing to be with her and to accept her.

Accepting the Person of the Child

This last point is very important in all applications of person centred theory. It seems paradoxical, but person centred theory proceeds from the assumption that change is more likely when a person's present way of being is understood and accepted. This refers to the underlying principle that the tendency towards full actualisation is an inherent characteristic, and that this tendency becomes operational in a climate of acceptance and understanding. Jeannette's job was not deliberately to change this child's behaviour into something more socially acceptable, but to offer Marie the psychological conditions that would enable her to change herself. Later, in reflecting on her work, Jeannette wrote:

The way of working I have described is essentially private. There are times when it is necessary for all of us to talk in confidence and to know that it will travel no further. However, I have worked with many children who have something to say in public. So often a child will know better than anyone exactly what she needs in order to thrive educationally and emotionally; but how often is the child seriously listened to and taken notice of? An aggressive child will be the absent subject of endless meetings with teachers and specialists and finally a decision will be made about the child's educational future. It is most likely that the decision arrived at will have more to do with alleviating the adults' anxiety than the real needs of the child. The provision will probably include some kind of exclusion; the child may spend part of the week out of school. The child is likely to regard the provision not as help but as punishment, reinforcing patterns long since formed of unacceptability and rejection. In the situation described in the story 'Marie', I was able to be the voice of the child and helped to enable her to stay in the school.

Play Therapy

Without labelling it as such, Jeanette's work with Marie took the form of a kind of play therapy. Virginia Axline (1969) has described play therapy as offering opportunities to children to experience personal growth under the best conditions possible. As children enact events in the form of play, feelings emerge for them to examine, control or resolve. Children thus realise their own power to become more independent thinkers and to become more psychologically mature.

A study of child centred play therapy with groups of young, bilingual Puerto-Rican children showed that child centred play therapy resulted in much less aggressive behaviour and more acceptance of others than would normally be expected (Trostle, 1988). The same study showed that the more developmentally advanced play level of 'reality-based play' was significantly higher for the children who received play therapy sessions than for those who did not. Interestingly, Trostle found that boys showed greater increases in feelings of acceptance towards others than did the girls involved in the study.

The Trostle study and the work of Jeannette Weaver have several things in common. They both show in their different ways the rewards of listening, as empathically as possible, to the ways in which children express themselves, whether this is in words or through behaviour. They also show how unhelpful it is to label children as failures, 'no-hopers', or 'difficult' in ways that then prevent adults from seeing the whole person of the child. In person centred terms, both of these pieces of work show that the actualising tendency, when given room to flourish, moves in ways that are creative and social.

Chapter 13
Can Schools Be More Caring?

So far we have considered individual experiences of school, and discussed how personal history plays a profoundly important part in the abilities of children to respond positively to their school experience. Part of the problem for the teacher is concerned with offering positive experiences to groups of children organised into classes. Groups are places where personal attention and consideration can be very hard to give and receive. Each individual child experiences personal attention some of the time, and observes the attention being given to others for the remainder of the time. The child responds to both parts of this experience – both direct and indirect.

Person centred teachers, and those naturally sympathetic to person centred ideas, face the constant problem of generating, within their classrooms, the kind of psychological environment that enables both the affective (emotional) side of children and the cognitive (intellectual) side to be nourished. As I have discussed earlier, these two sides of each person are not separate or unrelated. On entering the classroom, children do not put aside the concerns and anxieties they face in other aspects of their lives. Personal circumstances, family experiences and the like cannot be left at the door, but are brought right into the classroom and the school as a whole.

The person centred approach to education suggests that underlying attitudes, values and personal qualities are at least as important as technical skill in the job of teaching. In fact, the ideal situation would be one where teachers high in the facilitative attitudes discussed earlier are also highly skilled as teachers. The research evidence discussed in Chapter 11 points very firmly in this direction. The parallels between the worlds of therapy and teaching also begin to make more sense when we realise that the effective person centred therapist is someone who has internalised a set of facilitative attitudes and values that underpin their skills at communicating. The same is true of teaching, and to illustrate this I give an account from a teacher who clearly shares a person centred philosophy, and makes this apparent in everything he says about his experience of teaching in an urban primary school.

A Case Study

Geoffrey Court works alongside Jeannette Weaver at the Urban Learning Foundation in Tower Hamlets, a London inner city borough with tremendous social and economic difficulties. Geoffrey is the founder and main inspiration of the Schools Support Project, and has years of experience in primary teaching, including some time as a Deputy Head. His comments bring to life all of the theoretical issues we have discussed so far, especially in his description of the classroom as a place of care, respect, understanding and even love (Court, 1987). This account is in Geoffrey's own words.

> I've brought the register I used to use a year or two ago, with a class of nine and ten year olds. The register is an important document, not only because of its legal force (teachers are often reminded that this is a document which could be produced as evidence in a court of law), but because it is a central symbol of the class, in which every individual's name appears, and because taking the register, if it is done properly, is not just an administrative chore but an important ritual in which each child is recognised and greeted.
>
> The class in this register has long since dispersed into secondary schools, but the register is still significant for me. It's a reminder of the children with whom I spent five hours a day for forty weeks of the year. I remember them with a mixture of feelings, but above all with affection, and I'd like to spend a few minutes telling you about some of them.
>
> The register is about names, so let's start with a child who is confused about her name. Her own name, given to her by her own mother, was an African one; but when the child came to live with foster parents, they decided that an English name would be better. How this child felt about being separated from not only her natural mother but her name as well, I've no idea, but she was certainly very angry and destructive – the most difficult child I've ever had to handle.
>
> She had a friend in the class, who also had a reason to be confused about her origins ... Born to a young teenage mother, she has been rescued at the age of six months, filthy and covered in sores, by her grandmother, who had taken the child home on the bus and from then on raised the child as her own. Until a few months before I first met her, the child had been under the impression that her grandmother was her mother, and that her mother was her sister.
>
> Then there were a boy, his sister and their cousin, all of whom were finding it difficult to learn to read. They came from a family in which the only currency was violence. The children were encouraged, proudly and explicitly, to settle all matters with the fist, and to judge all people solely on their fighting ability. In this climate, the sister coped by sulking perpetually, the brother by escaping into a day-dream, and the cousin by alternating between precocious sexual behaviour and rage.
>
> If there were those whose style was violent, there were other children in this class who lived in fear: not specific fear, but general timidity. There

were five or six of them, and at one point timidity dissolved into sheer terror.

First, it's necessary to explain that the school has a Partially Hearing Unit which is fully integrated; that is to say the children are very much treated as members of the whole school community and participate in all its activities.

We took a group of hearing and partially hearing children to Wales for a week of outdoor pursuits, and one afternoon we went caving. Caves, as you may or may not know, are wet places, and they can also be very resonant, so we advised the partially hearing children to take their hearing aids off. Accompanied, of course, by a caving expert, we set off on our underground walk, though perhaps slide, bump, wade, crawl and shiver would be better words than walk. Half-way, we came to the biggest challenge of the expedition. There was a ledge along which we had to pull ourselves on our stomachs – the ceiling was only eighteen inches above the floor. The ledge was just wide enough for one person: on the left was a wall of rock, and on the right a sheer drop with icy water at the bottom.

The child in question got half-way along the ledge before he panicked. We could tell that he had panicked because he stopped, went rigid and started to wail. Reassurance was clearly called for, and this posed a challenge to our professional abilities which for me has never been equalled, before or since. The teacher in front couldn't turn round. The teacher behind couldn't move forward because there were other children in the way who couldn't move either. We couldn't speak to the child because he'd taken his hearing aids off, and in any case he was wailing loudly.

Well, of course, I've made it sound much worse than it really was. We had an expert with us, and he simply climbed sideways along the vertical face above the water, and coaxed the child out of his panic. There was no actual danger, and I have put the story in as much for light relief as anything. On the other hand, though, we had glimpsed in an extreme form the kind of fear which some children carry with them, as timidity or insecurity, through most of their waking lives.

Back to the class. There were three more children who will remain in my memory until I die. The first was a girl of considerable ability, whose family background was full of ambiguity and violence. Her mother had a friend whose cohabitee was in prison and whose own daughter was in care, so Lorna (that's what I'll call her, though it isn't her name) had taken to visiting this woman and staying the night. One morning, Lorna came in and told me she had nearly burned to death. She had been sleeping on the floor in front of an electric fire, and the eiderdown began to smoulder. The friend with whom Lorna was staying had to throw water over her to put the fire out. Lorna also used to talk about a man whom she used to visit, and who took his trousers down. At the age of ten or eleven she was quite evidently using drugs of some description, too. I felt angry and helpless on the days when this once alert child seemed dazed and unable to put two thoughts together.

The second member of this final trio of children also lived in a vague wilderness like Lorna's. He would cycle two miles at the end of the day, and see whether his father's light was on. If it was, he would stay there; if not he would return to his mother's to sleep. He was always extremely dirty from head to foot. He was an accomplished burglar at eleven. Like Lorna, as time went on, he became more and more dazed in his manner.

The incident which alarmed me most concerned a good quality microscope which was the basis of much of the class's work for several weeks. Mark (I'll call him Mark) was more fascinated than most children by the microscopic world and had done some excellent work – he was a gifted artist. One morning, a part of the microscope was missing, and it couldn't be used. After a time-consuming search, it was revealed that Mark had taken it and thrown it in the bushes. This piece of paradoxical behaviour was a nice example of the tendency of some children to undermine the activity of the classroom, even when they are finding it really enjoyable.

The last child I'd like to talk about looks like the European stereotype of the cathedral choirboy. Blue eyes, blond hair, impish features. He is the biggest rogue in the neighbourhood, and I failed utterly to engage him. The youngest of the family, he was indulged hopelessly by his parents, who refused to see any wrong in him. We were lucky if he came to school on one day out of ten, so in a sense you might think I would only have had to worry about him for ten per cent of the time; but, of course, he was still in my class, I still felt responsible for him. Nevertheless, there is a limit to the number of times you can search the streets for a child who might literally be anywhere. He spent his time with eighteen or nineteen year olds, the kind of adolescents who would pay him to distribute National Front literature. The had introduced him to the pleasures of tobacco and alcohol and probably other drugs. Like Mark, he was and is and active burglar. In trouble with the police at the age of nine, he knocked on the door of an elderly witness and threatened her so effectively that she withdrew her evidence. The child demonstrated brilliantly that if you are defiant enough, it is possible to run rings round the whole legal process, at least until you are old enough to go to prison – or your life-style kills you.

The funniest example of this child's attitude was his response to a very large and very powerful headteacher. He's only a little squirt, this child, but his line was, 'I hope you like hospital food, 'cos that's what you're gonna be eating.'

These, then, are some of the children with whom I spent my days as a class teacher. The point is, they didn't leave their rage, their anxiety, their destructive impulses, their confusion outside the classroom door, like a pair of muddy wellingtons. They brought the whole lot in with them. Neither did they come in with a view of school as a source of growth, a way forward. In their hearts, most of them came believing, as their parents did, that school was somewhere you were sent by law, in order to learn that you were a failure.

It's at this point that I would like to make a number of things clear. The first is that, of course, there were children of another kind as well, children who might be described as miraculous. The girl who got her four younger brothers and sisters up in the morning, fed them and probably dressed them, and was forgiven if she was a few minutes late for school. The partially hearing child whose dignity, grace, warmth and sensitivity were an example to most adults. The boy whose playing of the violin was as soulful as his eyes. I don't want to give the impression that all Tower Hamlets children are hurt, or angry – far from it, though I do have a hunch that there are more such children in inner-city areas than elsewhere. The trouble is, it has to be a hunch because emotional deprivation can't be measured in the way that physical deprivation perhaps can.

I also want to make it clear that I do not wish to condemn these children, or their parents. That would be an impertinence. Neither do I express pity; some of these children are more worldly, more self-sufficient than I shall ever be. Still less do I want to complain about having to teach this class; I loved the children, which is not to say that there weren't days when I could cheerfully have clouted them; I loved the work, which is not to say that it wasn't exhausting and frustrating a lot of the time; and much of what we did together gave all of us great pleasure. In telling you the story of some of these children, my aim is simply to describe a bit of what it means, for me, to be a Tower Hamlets primary teacher.

Now it's self-evident that I haven't yet mentioned the issue which stands at the centre of the work of many of my colleagues, and informs all that they do in school: the question of appropriate provision for the substantial population in Tower Hamlets of children from Bangladesh. Although, like all teachers – I repeat, all teachers – I have a clear active responsibility to educate children for life in a multicultural society, and will take an explicit anti-racist stand even if this means upsetting some parents, I do not have experience of working in a school where the language and culture of most of the children are different from my own. Of course, I have friends who do work in such schools, and I can pass on some of the things I have heard them say. They've mentioned, for example, how isolated and excluded they can feel when they can't understand what the children are saying to one another. This raises questions about whether these children should be taught by people who do understand their language, and that in turn raises issues to do with teacher training and supply.

Another dilemma is the commitment I have to equal opportunity for all, and to redressing the imbalance which puts girls at a disadvantage. Some Bangladeshi parents will not share this view, and indeed may actively disagree with it. Where does this leave the teacher in the front line? Is it racist to challenge the parents' deeply and sincerely held opinions?

I started by writing about a difficult class. I had a good year with that class, during which a lot of learning and growing went on for all of us. This was only possible, though, because the headteacher of the school had worked for years to make it a caring and supportive place. I had help and encouragement from my colleagues, as I hope they did from me, and I was allowed to try new approaches if the old ones were failing. The level of discussion amongst the staff was high, and the power in the place was shared to a large extent. Not all teachers are lucky enough to work in such a place, and many, especially at the moment, are feeling alone and dispirited.

Geoffrey's values and attitudes towards the children in his class are revealed in the first paragraph when he writes about the register, '... not just an administrative chore, but an important ritual in which each child is recognised and greeted'. He is doing whatever he can, at the start of each day, to acknowledge and relate to each child as an individual, with a personal place within the group. That he values each child is further revealed by his feelings about Lorna, 'I felt angry and helpless when this once alert child seemed dazed and unable to put two thoughts together'. The point that we raised at the beginning of this chapter, that children bring their emotional selves into the classroom is underlined, '... they didn't leave their rage, their anxiety, their destructive impulses, their confusion outside the classroom door, like a pair of muddy wellingtons'.

The Values of the School

A most significant point that Geoffrey makes concerns the attitudes and qualities of the headteacher of this school, who '... had worked for years to make it a caring and supportive place'. This comment reflects one made by Rogers (1983), who observed that for a person centred approach to exist in any school there was one precondition:

> The precondition is: a leader or a person who is perceived as an authority figure in the situation is sufficiently secure within herself and in her relationship to others that she experiences an essential trust in the capacity of others to think for themselves, to learn for themselves (p. 188).

If this precondition existed, Rogers thought that a number of consequences would follow, and we leave this chapter by quoting him

> In meetings of the class or of the school as a whole, an atmosphere of realness, of caring, and of understanding listening is evident. This climate may spring initially from the person who is the perceived leader. As the learning process continues, it is more and more often provided by the learners for each other. Learning from each other becomes as important as learning from books or films or work experiences (pp. 188–9).

Chapter 14
Can School Students Really Be Trusted?

Many times in this book, the idea that people can be trusted to choose positive and meaningful directions for themselves has arisen. This is clearly an optimistic view of human nature, and it cannot be denied that there are many occasions in which the opposite seems to be true – when people behave violently and destructively towards themselves and others. The person centred view of this – that destructive behaviour stems from the internalisation of negative conditions of worth – is discussed more fully elsewhere in this book. Incorporating negative conditions of worth into our self-concept is a form of learning; we learn from others more powerful than ourselves who we are supposed to be, and how much worth we have. The 'self' which we then try to actualise becomes a damaged and conditional self. The true self (the organismic self) has become buried under layers of conditions of worth.

If those on whom we depend for survival relate to us in ways that trust our capacity for self-actualisation, the 'true' self will have more chance to develop and find expression in the world in creative and positive ways. Most conventional education tends to operate on the assumption that children need to be controlled rather than liberated. Person centred psychology argues in favour of introducing more democratic, cooperative values in schools, and regarding academic attainment and the development of social responsibility and self-knowledge as equally important. These are central values in humanistic education, and have been widely supported by humanistically oriented educators for a long time. James Hemming, for example, put these sentiments very strongly:

> A deeply damaging hypocrisy of the school that treats academic attainment as its primary value is that, however much it may talk of *esprit de corps* on the playing field, or in out-of-school activities, the principle for the classroom is *esprit de moi* – the egocentric, competitive drive. In schools, as in industry, it is an illusion that competition is what achieves results. Competition is always divisive in its ultimate consequences. Competition is

a stimulus but it is cooperation that gets things done. The community role of an individual is to contribute what he, or she, has to give in the setting of cooperative purpose. A modern education should be concerned with developing together individual achievement and social contribution (Hemmings, 1980: 90).

Learning cooperatively in groups where there is a sense of interdependence rather than competition is, however, an approach used in many schools, with encouraging results. One study (Johnson et al., 1981) reviewed 122 research studies into the effects of cooperative learning. It found:

1. Students achieve more in cooperative interaction than when in competition with each other.
2. Cooperation seems to be powerful in producing achievement, and results hold for several subject areas and age groups.
3. Students are more positive about school, subject areas and teachers.
4. Students are more positive about each other when they learn cooperatively, regardless of differences in ability, ethnic background etc.
5. Students are more effective interpersonally. Students with cooperative experiences are more able to take the perspective of others, are more positive about taking part in controversy, have better developed interaction skills, and have a more positive expectation about working with other students than students from competitive or individualistic settings.

One way of treating children democratically and with trust is to find ways of involving them more directly in their own learning. This is sometimes referred to as *experiential learning* – learning through experience. Experiential learning, according to Carl Rogers:

> *has a quality of personal involvement* – the whole person in both feeling and cognitive aspects being in the learning event. It is *self-initiated*. Even when the impetus or stimulus comes from the outside, the sense of discovery, of reaching out, of grasping and comprehending, comes from within. *It is pervasive*. It makes a difference in the behaviour, the attitudes, perhaps even the personality of the learner. *It is evaluated by the learner*. She knows whether it is meeting her need, whether it leads towards what she *wants* to know, whether it illuminates the dark area of ignorance she is experiencing. The locus of evaluation, we might say, resides definitely in the learner. *Its essence is meaning*. When such learning takes place, the element of meaning to the learner is built into the whole experience (Rogers, 1983: 20).

A Case Study – The Village Project

To illustrate this, what follows is an example of experiential learning among a group of 44 school students aged twelve to thirteen. The example comes from King Alfred School in London, where Stephen de

Brett, the Design and Technology teacher, had the idea of the 'Village Project'. The general aim of this project was to provide the students with a person centred experience of living and learning together in a way not possible in the confines of the classroom. An important aspect was that students would be involved in making decisions and choices that were real, unlike so much classroom teaching which is simulated or abstract.

The Village Project consisted of the students designing and building a village community in which they would then live for an entire week during term time, with all other teaching suspended. Because they had to live in the results of their designing and making, it mattered what they did. If their huts were poorly thought out, they would leak, fall down or just be uncomfortable. The students were responsible for making all the major decisions that affected them, like what time to sleep, when to get up, what to cook, when to work and play, and how to keep order within the village. The students, then, had a large measure of control in creating their own world in which they could experiment with some of the most fundamental aspects of that world. The staff role was restricted to making the village safe enough for the students to try things out and make mistakes.

The students formed themselves into groups to design their own living accommodation for the week. The materials chosen were straw for thatched roofs and willow for wattle walls. The frames were made from birch poles – thinnings from a nearby wood. The students cut the trees with the foresters who then showed them how to weave these raw materials into usable walls. The students also met in groups to organise various aspects of the village. For example, one group organised food buying, another discussed how the village community should make decisions, and whether they wanted a leader, a governing council or a leaderless village. Another group invented a complex legal system during one of their English lessons, but their idea was rejected by the others who had not been part of the discussion. The students struggled to make decisions and learned some valuable lessons about democracy. The political model adopted eventually was that of a leaderless community. Decisions were made by the whole village meeting together with a different chairperson for each meeting.

Every student was encouraged to produce something to represent their time in the village. An exhibition of this work included chalk carvings, teas made from leaves found on the site, hammocks, bags, diaries and wall hangings. One student who had watched the science teacher demonstrate hammock making became fascinated by the knots used, and spent the rest of the week studying the principle of knots.

After the project was over, the staff asked for an evaluation to be made of it by an outside person who had not previously been involved. This evaluation (Fairhurst, 1990) highlighted some of the learning and some of the disappointments that had arisen for the children during the week. One of the most important things that emerged from the evaluation was how much the students had appreciated being listened to by the teachers, and having their opinions and points of view taken seriously. They talked in terms of 'being trusted', and some said they felt good about realising they could take responsibility for themselves because, before the project started, they did not think they would be able to.

The learning took many different forms, some children talking about freedom of choice, or learning about things like anger and frustration, while others talked about learning specific skills like cooking, or making things out of natural materials. The difficulties inherent in such an unusual situation also contained valuable learning for the children. For example, the process of forming small groups was experienced as very difficult by some of the children, and one girl thought her relationships with some of the other girls had suffered. Another girl said she had learned how important it was to listen to other people's points of view before making up her mind about situations, and also said she had learned not to be so 'soft' and willing to please.

Experiential learning of the kind described here involves the whole person in the learning process. Emotional responses to situations and people are valued as highly as the information or 'facts' that make up the overt curriculum. A feature of the Village Project was the democratic, cooperative values that inspired it, values that are built-in to this school's way of approaching the whole of the educational process. The ideas that inspired the Village Project are echoed and supported by Richards and Richards (1988):

> At the heart of a humanistic vision of education is a commitment to educational processes and practices that give major emphasis to the optimal development of the individual and the human community. Humanistic educators seek to establish a learning climate that is perceived by all involved as meaningful, challenging, supportive, and free from abusiveness, threat or victimisation. Further, the goals and principles of humanistic education are central to the ideals of a democratic way of life.

I am not trying to give the impression that the problems faced by schools and individual teachers are not complex, or that there are easy solutions. Neither am I meaning to give the impression that experiential learning, or even total student choice about what to learn, are, in themselves, complete solutions. I am reminded of the comments made by Wood (1986), a close colleague of Carl Rogers:

> The student's personal choice in what to study should not be exaggerated. It is necessary to learn some facts and information before one has an interest in the subject. This point was painfully demonstrated in the recent disaster at a Soviet nuclear power station. A person received very serious injuries

from radiation while bicycling in a contaminated area. Particularly in matters of survival one cannot wait until his interest is aroused to learn the threats that surround him. One must understand (without indulging in unnecessary fear) the dangerous effects of radioactivity or the breeding habits of disease-carrying mosquitoes or the dangers of polluted air before a problem is manifested – otherwise, when the problem appears it is frequently already too late to prevent disaster.

Society has the responsibility for educational systems which prepare its citizens for known eventualities, and, now, perhaps even unknown eventualities. The educational system has a responsibility to know what it wants its students to learn, beyond merely the skill of going to school. The person-centred approach must accommodate learning for eventualities known and unknown, and learning which is *less* personalised as well as more personalised.

The point is to provide an educational system that enables intellectual activity to happen alongside the development of emotional security and social responsibility. Rogers, and other humanistic or 'progressive' educators, offered a way of thinking about teaching and learning that contrasts (sometimes sharply) with the more traditional or conventional view. To them, this means that the attitudes and values that are expressed in schools, from the way the school organises its business, to the way teachers form relationships with classes and individual children, need to be radically revised.

I hope, that in the foregoing chapters, I have given you some insights into the kinds of things that humanistic educators see as essential if schools are to become more of what most people want them to be – places where children are valued and nurtured, and where their learning about the world includes becoming more sensitive to the similarities and differences between people and cultures.

Section IV
Culture, Groups, Power and Peace

There are two themes running through the three chapters in this final section. Firstly, we move closer to 'real life' situations where person centred psychology is making a significant contribution. This develops the theme we started in the previous section on education – that person centred psychology is a 'living psychology' interested in philosophical questions and the development of individual potential, *and* attempts to understand people in the varied social contexts in which they live their lives.

The second theme is the more subtle question of power, the way it is distributed and how it is used and abused. Traditionally, political power has been used to control, exploit and constrain individuals and groups. Relationships existing within an authoritarian power structure are 'based on the belief that some person, nation, political or economic group, race or gender is superior to another, and that the inferior participant in the relationship needs to be controlled, manipulated or directed' (Natiello, 1990). In the final chapter there is a discussion of 'collaborative power', a quite different way of looking at personal and political power.

In the first of the three chapters, I explore how cultural influences affect the capacity of people to understand and help each other. So often, people whose intention is to help others are experienced as patronising, uncomprehending and sometimes insensitive or even racist. In a culture in which 'helpers' are likely to be the more fortunate, or who come from (and are seen to represent) the more powerful groups in that culture, there seems to be a certain inevitability about this. But it need not remain this way, and there is now a growing sensitivity to these issues, and a determination to do something about them.

Person centred psychology has a real, and I think underestimated, contribution to make here. Several times in this book I have touched on questions and issues that are related to power and its distribution. This is most clearly seen in the chapter on person centred psychotherapy. The more traditional attitude is to place power in the hands of the 'expert' and to rely on his (because it is usually a 'he') greater knowledge and technique to lead a troubled patient towards health. In accepting this as the proper way to do things, we are in danger of giving up our own capacities to heal ourselves, and handing them over to others.

This represents the 'medical model', but even in matters of physical health there are changes happening. Childbirth, for example, was once treated as if it were an illness. Contact between the mother and the process of childbirth was disrupted by well-meaning medical experts legitimately concerned for the health and welfare of mother and child. Natural childbirth, birth without violence and the 'Leboyer method' are now widespread practices in which childbirth is seen as a wholly natural process, not a medical crisis.

In person centred therapy we can see a substantial shift in the way power is distributed between therapist and client, and this shift of power is echoed in the relationship between a person centred group and its 'facilitator'. This is the subject of Chapter 16 – how person centred psychology has developed an approach to group work. In this chapter I explore the 'basic encounter group' which consists (usually) of 'well functioning' people who want to discover more about themselves and their relationships. The two examples given are of groups that had other purposes as well. In the first example the group consisted of young people preparing to live for a while in a different country. In the second, the group had a political purpose connected with the situation in South Africa at the time. I chose these two groups deliberately – to show how person centred psychology looks outwards from the individual to the wider social, political and economic reality.

The last chapter in this book ventures even further out into the world, and tackles one of the most challenging questions of our times – can we learn to live in peace with one another? This question occupied much of Carl Rogers' time towards the end of his life. His 'peace work' took him to South Africa, Ireland, the USSR (as it was then), Hungary and many other troubled places. Wherever he went, he worked to apply the person centred principles he had committed himself to from very early in his professional life. In this chapter issues of complex political power arise time and again.

I started this book with some 'philosophical' questions about human nature and individual experience. I then focused on the application of person centred psychology to a particular social setting – education. There are other areas in which the person centred approach has made a contribution: to management and administration, to social work and youth work, and in medical settings, for example. I hope, if you are interested, you will follow up on these areas for yourself. I finish the book in much the same way that Carl Rogers finished his life – with a concern for the continuation of human life on this vulnerable

Earth, and with the hope that person centred psychology can continue to make more contributions to interpersonal and international peace and understanding.

Chapter 15
Can Person Centred Psychology Work in a Multicultural Society?

So far in this book I have written, in the main, about relationships between individual people. I have said that listening, understanding and striving for genuineness and acceptance are the keys to clear and effective communication. Whilst I believe this to be true, I also know that understanding others depends on a willingness to acknowledge the differences in culture, history and expectations between ourselves and those whose experiences are different from ours. For example, Sue (1981) discusses issues relating to cross-cultural counselling by posing a number of questions, for example: what is cross-cultural counselling; is it any different from other forms of counselling; can someone of one race or culture effectively counsel someone from a different race or culture, and what might be some of the obstacles to effective cross-cultural counselling?

The 'Western' Bias in Theories of Helping

It is now generally understood that most theories of counselling and psychotherapy are derived from Western culture and, therefore, may not always be useful in other cultural settings (e.g. McFadden, 1988; Pederson, 1987). In Britain many cultural groups coexist, sometimes uneasily. In Chapter 13 we saw how issues of race, culture and language have become day-to-day concerns for teachers working in schools where many languages are spoken. A very important consideration for all counsellors (and, indeed, all 'helpers' such as nurses, teachers and social workers) is how far their efforts to understand others are affected by their own cultural norms, stereotypes and prejudices. D'Ardenne and Mahtani (1989), for example, point to the fact that Western ideas about self-exploration and self-determination 'create an intensity and exclusivity in the relationship which may be alien for a client from another culture' (p. 75). They argue that counsellors may not understand the ways some clients perceive themselves in relation to their family, community and culture.

111

The Bias of Academic Psychology

Bimrose (1993) points out that counselling has its roots in the academic discipline of psychology, and in seeking to understand human behaviour, psychology begins at the individual level:

> As a result, therefore, of deriving from this particular academic tradition, counselling theory locates explanations relating to the client's need for help within the individual. In so doing, these theories separate an individual's need for help, however this is manifested, from their social context, and thus define social context as irrelevant to the counselling process (p. 155).

Bimrose puts the work of Carl Rogers firmly within this academic tradition, 'One of Rogers' central ideas is that individuals are able to determine their own destinies. Thus, control lies within the individual, rather than externally in the social context' (p. 156). I think this is a fair point to make. It is certainly true that, at least in his early years as a practitioner, Rogers concerned himself with understanding individuals and their experiences, and did not explicitly include considerations of their social context in his books and articles. Later, however, Rogers did become much more concerned with the 'politics' of counselling and psychotherapy, especially when he moved into the cross-cultural work I describe in Chapter 17. Ponterotto and Benesch (1988) believe that Rogers' approach, in placing so much importance on the personal qualities of therapists, is able to overcome cultural boundaries successfully because the therapist is concerned to understand the experiences of all clients, which would include experiences influenced by culture and social context.

Pedersen (1987) believes that one area of cultural bias is the assumption that what is 'normal' to one group is also 'normal' to any other. He thinks that what is normal changes according to the situation and the cultural background of the person being judged. He warned against the dangers of diagnostic mistakes when definitions of normality that belong to one culture are applied to people of other cultures. According to Usher (1989):

> Rogers seems to have recognised this source of bias, having made objections himself to therapists making diagnoses of clients based on their own evaluations.
>
> Furthermore, psychological diagnosis 'has certain social and philosophical implications which ... are undesirable. When the locus of evaluation is seen as residing in the expert, it would appear that the long range social implications are in the direction of the social control of the many by the few' (Rogers, 1951, p. 224) It seems, then, that Rogers avoided this source of bias by espousing the view that only the individual, embedded in a particular social, cultural, and historical context, could define 'normal' behaviour for himself or herself.

However, Usher (1989) goes on to criticise Rogers, and by implication many approaches to helping others, on a number of grounds. Like Bimrose, Usher believes that Rogers was 'heavily dependent on the general field of psychology and did not incorporate the salience of cultural issues in counselling'. Usher also believes that many of the terms used by Rogers, such as 'congruence' and 'genuineness' might be 'difficult to understand for people of cultures that do not value subjective experience, deep levels of self-awareness and insight, or close, revealing relationships'. Similarly, words or phrases like 'self-actualisation', 'self-awareness' and 'self-direction' are examples of Rogers' emphasis on individual development and may be 'in opposition to the values in some cultures of negation of the self, for example, in the Hindu culture. (Hindus do not strive for self-enhancement but, rather, oneness with a greater Being.)' In defence of Rogers, though, Usher thinks that:

> ... because Rogers left the definition of these 'self' goals up to each individual, a client from a particular cultural context could define for himself or herself what behavioural or attitudinal changes would constitute moving toward 'self-actualisation', as he or she defined it (p. 66).

Rogers believed that the Person Centred Approach was less liable to cultural bias than other forms of helping because it did not depend on helpers making evaluations of their clients. In person centred therapy, for example, clients define the goals for themselves, and therapists try to understand the world as their clients see and experience it. However, person centred therapy, with its emphasis on individual experience, and its dependence on clients' ability and willingness to talk about feelings, does run the risk of finding it difficult to help people whose cultural norms are not so 'individualistic'.

Cultural Perceptions of Counselling and Psychotherapy

The ways in which cultural groups see the role of counselling in their lives, and the ways in which they are used to communicating with others, may also determine the extent to which some people can be helped by counselling. For example, Waxer (1989) found that Cantonese students, asked to read transcripts of Rogers counselling clients, were less interested in seeing Rogers as their counsellor than were Canadian students who read the same transcripts. Waxer thought that this was because Cantonese people view counselling as more 'directive, paternalistic and autocratic' than Canadian people who see it as more ' explorative and democratic'.

The Bias of Language

The language that helpers use, and how they make sense out of the language their clients use, can also be very important factors in determining whether clients experience them as helpful or not. Two examples will illustrate this. Lago and Thompson (1989) tell the following anecdote:

> This concerned a West Indian woman who arrived in Britain during the 1960s. She kept going to the labour exchange looking for a job. On her second or third visit, the woman behind the desk said 'I'm afraid we still haven't found a job for you.' The West Indian woman replied, strongly, 'I don't want you to be afraid of me, I want you to help me find a job' (p. 216).

Verhelst (1991) was a staff member at a workshop on the theme of 'cross-cultural communication and the PCA' in Sheffield, England in 1989. As a Flemish speaker, Verhelst says:

> I ... naturally identified with the participants of the other minority language groups. Furthermore, I felt uncomfortable when I perceived a lack of understanding and consideration by the native speakers for the language difficulties of the non-native speakers. Still to my own shock, I realised that I had the same degenerating attitude towards at least one particular participant belonging to a minority language group (p. 61).

Verhelst tells of how, in a group meeting, he encountered 'X', a Punjab Indian who speaks English as his second or third language. In the group, another participant spoke in a very personal and emotional way. X 'intervened and I perceived his intervention as not considerate at all. After a while, due to my growing irritation, I stopped X in a rather direct way.' However, X was assertive enough to continue speaking, and eventually expressed his care and concern for the previous speaker. After the session, Verhelst apologised to X and discussed what had happened. Verhelst discovered that in X's culture and mother-tongue, 'emotions are never expressed immediately, but they always follow a long, verbal introduction to prepare the other person!' Verhelst was able to think this incident through and, 'In particular I considered the manner in which I assumed that X (and others) think and perceive the world in the same way as I do, when they speak my language or a language that is familiar to me.'

The Problem of Racism

Communication (and understanding) is a complex process. The complexities and difficulties are bound to be multiplied when people come from different cultures and use language in such different ways. It is not just a 'technical' question, however, and issues of cultural stereotyping, prejudice, bias and racism also have a major part to play. Lago and Thompson (1989) remind us that, in the field of counselling (though the following sentiments could be expressed about all helpers):

> ... many white counsellors see themselves as caring, sensitive people who have chosen counselling precisely because they are concerned about other people. Therefore, they ask, how could they be racist in their practice? This genuinely held view does not take into account, however, a whole range of mechanisms, perceptions, and experiences to which white people have been exposed throughout their lives (p. 209).

According to McLeod (1993), 'Racism is part of the value system and fabric of contemporary society, and represents a factor of enormous importance for counselling. Counselling remains a predominantly "white" occupation, with relatively few black counsellors or black clients' (p. 116). Lago and Thompson (1989) discuss four 'scenarios' of counselling involving different racial pairings of counsellor and client – a white client with a black counsellor; a white counsellor with a black client; a white counsellor with a white client, and a black counsellor with a black client. They point to the different ways in which issues of race and ethnicity impinge on the counselling situations involved. For example, black counsellors are likely to have been trained by white, middle-class training organisations that are Eurocentric or American in origin and outlook. Consequently, black counsellors are 'geared to working with white people, not black people' (pp. 210–11). White counsellors with black clients are in danger of a 'perpetuation of the notion of white superiority. The white person, as the counsellor in this situation, has the power. The sensitive handling of that power is absolutely crucial' (p. 212).

Carl Rogers was aware from early in his career that cultural issues are important factors in helping relationships and, in discussing the training of counsellors, he wrote:

> It seems desirable that the student should have a broad experiential knowledge of the human being in his cultural setting ... Such knowledge needs to be supplemented by experiences of living with or dealing with individuals who have been the product of cultural influences very different from those which have molded the student. Such experience and knowledge often seem necessary to make possible the deep understanding of another (Rogers, 1951: 437).

Further Cultural Factors

The term 'multicultural' at the head of this chapter is not confined to issues of race and ethnicity. Bayne et al. (1994) use the term 'multiculturalism' which,

... emphasises a need for counsellors to be much more aware of differences in ethnic origin, gender, social class, disability, age and other factors... The multicultural approach contrasts with the traditional focus on individuals and on personality, which emphasises the possibility of change and development for everyone, regardless of multicultural factors, and in which counselling qualities, skills and strategies are seen as generally applicable (p. 101).

A fair charge against all approaches to counselling and other forms of helping is that they have been more meaningful and accessible to the dominant groups in society, and have not been so responsive to those who already are disadvantaged, or who experience discrimination in other walks of life (McLeod, 1993). The need for counsellors and other helpers to develop what Ridley et al. (1994) describe as 'cultural self-awareness' has never been greater. Helpers always bring to their work their own cultural values, beliefs and biases which affect the quality of the relationships they develop with their clients. Ridley et al. see cultural self-awareness as 'serving a similar function to Rogers' concept of congruence' (p. 260), and they think that 'culturally self-aware counsellors are more likely to facilitate client self-exploration, especially as it relates to their cultural identity' (p. 260).

Individuals differ a great deal from other people of the same culture and helpers need to be able to recognise these differences. Failing to recognise within-group differences can result in exaggerated stereotyping (Campbell, 1967) and, 'This may result in misdiagnosis, identification of inappropriate outcome goals, and treatment selection errors. Moreover, communication of these stereotypes in counselling may evoke mistrust in the client and cause premature termination' (Ridley et al., 1994: 261).

Social Class

Middle-class people are more likely to look for counselling than are people from working-class backgrounds. Counsellors and psychotherapists are often middle-class themselves and are used to working with people from similar backgrounds. Middle-class people are possibly more determined to find a counsellor, and are more likely to be able to afford it.

Gender

Apart from social class and ethnicity, McLeod identifies three other major areas where some people or groups of people are likely to experience disadvantage. The first of these concerns gender, and McLeod points out that 'virtually all of the key historical figures in counselling and psychotherapy have been men, and they have written, whether consciously or not, from a male perspective' (McLeod, 1993: 111). Some exceptions are Anna Freud, Karen Horney and Alice Miller. Recently, there have been attempts to construct feminist approaches to counselling and psychotherapy, described by Llewelyn and Osborne (1983) as based on four assumptions about the social experience of women:

1. Women are consistently in a position of deference to men. For example, women tend to have less power or status in work situations.
2. Women are expected to be aware of the feelings of others, and to supply emotional nurturing to others, especially men.
3. Women are expected to be 'connected' to men, so that the achievement of autonomy is difficult.
4. The issue of sexuality is enormously problematic for women. This factor arises from a social context in which images of idealised women's bodies are used to sell commodities, assertive female sexuality is threatening to many men, and sexual violence against women is widespread (from McLeod, 1993: 113–114).

None of the above remarks mean that men do not also face enormously complex problems concerning their gender roles or feelings about themselves as men. Recently, according to Chaplin (1989), there have been developments in men's awareness of their own gender related issues:

> And for men there are increasing numbers of films and television programmes showing men who express the so-called 'feminine' side of themselves. Counsellors can refer to these images and they can also be models themselves of people who can express both 'masculine' and 'feminine' characteristics. Most male counsellors do seem to have accepted their own 'feminine' side to some extent or they would not be engaged in such a caring, so-called 'female' type of profession of themselves (pp. 234–5).

Sexual Orientation

It was not until 1974 that homosexuality was no longer regarded as a psychiatric disorder by the American Psychiatric Association. In a culture that still stigmatises sexual orientations that are different from the majority, gay, lesbian and bisexual people will continue to experience emotional problems that are a direct result of the way others think about them and act towards them. The person centred approach, while seeing all sexual orientations as equally worthy of acceptance and understanding, has not really confronted the complex issues that are involved. Rogers (1973) in *On Becoming Partners* wrote quite extensively about sexual relationships, but did not explore (and hardly mentioned) relationships between homosexual partners.

Religion

A major source of problems for helpers can be the fact that their clients hold radically different religious beliefs from their own, and it can be difficult for helpers to take this fact into account. We have already seen that counselling, including to some extent person centred counselling, emphasises individual responsibility and action, and that this may conflict sharply with beliefs that emphasise, for example, the importance of the influence of God. Stereotypes about religious beliefs, or the outright rejection of religious creeds by a helper, will influence the extent to which the helper is able to empathise with the client. Our multicultural society includes people from all the world's religions, but counselling theorists and practitioners have not, in general, incorporated this fact in theories of effectiveness.

Is Person Centred Psychology Effective in a Multicultural Society?

There cannot be an unequivocal answer to this question. To say 'Yes' would be to ignore the very real problems I have discussed in brief in this chapter, and to assert that the PCA has confronted and resolved them all. This is clearly not the case. To say 'No' would be to take the most pessimistic line, and would ignore all the contributions that person centred psychology has made and is making to the development of effective theory and practice.

The most honest answer is to say 'Yes and No', and to acknowledge strengths while recognising weaknesses. The weaknesses include a lack of theory in respect of particular social and cultural groups. Carl Rogers did not emphasise the need to develop approaches that took specific cultural factors into account, but this is partly explained by the person centred view that 'what is personal is universal'. In other words, that the differences between people are outweighed by the similarities, and that understanding, empathy and acceptance are activities (or qualities) that transcend cultural and social differences.

These days, there are 'tailor made' approaches to counselling, for example, with gay people, people from different ethnic origins, different social classes, and so on. In general, person centred psychology has not developed similar specific approaches to deal with these and other social and economic factors, though awareness of potential problems is developing rapidly. For example, all substantial training courses in person centred counselling now include social context factors as a matter of good practice. Bimrose (1993) welcomes the general trend in counsellor training towards considering social context issues more closely and concludes:

If this succeeds in increasing the level of debate by raising levels of awareness, the quality of counselling practice, in the longer term, can only be enhanced (p. 164).

D'Ardenne and Mahtani (1989) remind us that change in counselling is, at its best, a two way process. Counsellors can be changed by their experiences with their clients, and Rogers was particularly keen that person centred counsellors should be as open to the possibilities for change as their clients.

Counsellors come face to face not only with their clients' experience of prejudice, restricted economic and social opportunities, but also the wealth of their family life, their language and traditions. From this, counsellors grow in their understanding of the additional effort and complexity involved in their clients communicating across cultures (D'Ardenne and Mahtani, 1989: 100–1).

The strengths of the PCA in this context lie in its philosophical attitude towards people, human nature and the possibilities for change. Being 'person centred' involves attempts to understand people from within their own frames of reference, to see the world as they see it, and to share in it without judgement. The fact that person centred psychology does not view labelling people as a useful activity, and avoids 'diagnosing' them from a culturally determined viewpoint of what constitutes 'normal', is a strength when it comes to encountering people from different cultures.

Chapter 16
Does Person Centred Psychology Work with Groups?

Person centred psychology has always been interested in groups – what happens in them, how they can be made more effective, and how they can be used to help people become more fully functioning. In the person centred approach, encounter groups have long been used as a way of promoting personal growth, and as a way of helping people explore conflicts and difficulties. Rogers and Sanford (1980) made a useful distinction between encounter groups and therapy groups:

> If persons come together because they are seeking help with serious problems, it is termed group therapy; if their purpose is to enrich and enhance their own development, it may be called an encounter group; but the process is much the same (Rogers and Sanford, 1980).

Encounter groups may meet only once for a few hours or, more usually, for two hours or so every week for several weeks. They offer opportunities for people to focus on aspects of their lives that are creating concern or anxiety, and groups are often good places for experimenting with new, more satisfying behaviours and ways of relating to others. They are called encounter groups to signify that their purpose is for individuals to do more than just meet and talk with each other in the everyday sense. The word 'encounter' implies a deeper meeting with more personal contact among people than usually happens in everyday life.

Encounter groups usually have a 'facilitator' – someone whose role is to help establish and maintain a climate of empathic listening, authenticity and positive regard. The facilitator's role is similar to that of the individual counsellor or therapist; he or she tries to listen carefully and with empathy, and to offer respect and caring as genuinely as possible. Facilitators of person centred encounter groups are happy to follow whatever direction the group may take, and to acknowledge feelings as they are expressed, whether these feelings are positive or so-called negative ones. Their aim is to work towards the creation of a climate of safety and trust, and this is better achieved by *being* empathic and caring than by *talking* about empathy and caring. Devonshire (1991) has described the role of the group facilitator in the following terms:

> When the facilitator can enter into the experience with others as a *learner*, rather than as a teacher or a psychological technician and can put aside his or her own convictions as to what individuals or the group *should do, should be, or should feel*, then a unique experience is most likely for all involved. When a facilitator with these attitudes and values is *being with* the group, then improved interpersonal communication and understanding almost always emerge; growth seems to come as a result of the greater inter- action among members of the group and is not merely a result of the skill and techniques of the 'expert' (p. 24).

The Facilitator and the Question of Power

As with individual therapy, a central issue for group facilitators to address is the question of power. It is undeniable that facilitators have more power in the group than other participants, perhaps simply because they are the most experienced person in groups present, or through the power that other participants confer on them. How facilita- tors deal with this question is partly a function of the degree to which they have adopted and internalised the facilitative attitudes and quali- ties of empathy, congruence and positive regard, and partly to do with how well they have resolved needs to manipulate or direct others. However, because the person centred style of encounter group does not rely on techniques or methods that are manipulative or directive, the power issue is not as critical as it can be in groups that rely on sug- gestion, persuasion or some sort of confrontation between the facilita- tor and other group participants.

Another reason why questions of power are so important stems from experiences of being in encounter groups in which people describe how they feel their own 'right to be' has been taken from them by people more powerful than they. An encounter group can be a place where people can discover what it means to be more personally authentic or congruent. This especially applies to people who, in their everyday life, feel obliged to play some sort of role, to pretend to be different from who they really are, or who feel compelled to repress genuine feelings. If, in an encounter group, such people can discover the courage to emerge from behind defensive barriers, even for a short time, then they are more likely to be able to incorporate more authen- tic 'ways of being' into their daily lives. A facilitator who encourages only certain kinds of behaviour, or only some expressions of self or a limited range of feelings, may simply be repeating the conditions which many people have experienced in the outside world.

What Happens in Encounter Groups?

Person centred encounter groups usually contain between six and twenty-four participants, plus one or more facilitators. At the beginning, they can feel awkward, with no-one really knowing what is expected of them, or what is going to happen. Groups seem to go through a number of stages in their development, which have been described by Carl Rogers (1970), and are summarised here:

1. *Milling around*: the facilitator makes it clear at the outset that this is a group with unusual freedom and that he or she will not take directional responsibility; there tends to develop a period of initial confusion, awkward silence, polite surface interaction, 'cocktail-party talk', frustration and a marked lack of continuity.

2. *Resistance to personal expression or exploration*: during the milling period, some individuals are likely to reveal some rather personal attitudes. This tends to foster very ambivalent reactions among other members of the group.

3. *Description of past feelings*: in spite of ambivalence about the trustworthiness of the group, expression of feelings does gradually begin to assume a larger proportion of the discussion.

4. *Expression of negative feelings*: curiously enough, the first expression of genuinely significant here-and-now feelings is apt to come out in negative attitudes towards other group members or toward the facilitator.

5. *Expression and exploration of personally meaningful material*: given the events in stage 4, it seems strange that the event most likely to occur next is for individuals to reveal themselves to the group in significant ways. The reason for this, no doubt, is that they have come to realise that this is, in part, their group. They can make out of it what they wish. They have also experienced the fact that negative feelings have been expressed and have usually been accepted or assimilated without any catastrophic results. They realise that there is freedom here, albeit a risky freedom. A climate of trust is beginning to develop. Now group members begin to take chances and to gamble with letting others know some deeper facets of themselves.

6. *The expression of immediate interpersonal feelings in the group*: entering into the process sometimes earlier, sometimes later, is the explicit move by one group member to express feelings experienced in the immediate moment towards another group member; these feelings are sometimes positive, sometimes negative.

7. *The development of a healing capacity in the group*: One of the most fascinating aspects of any intensive group experience is the manner in which a number of group members show a natural and spontaneous capacity for dealing in a helpful, facilitative and therapeutic fashion with the pain and suffering of others.

8. *Self-acceptance and the beginning of change*: It is believed by some people that self-acceptance stands in the way of change. In these person centred group experiences, however (as in psychotherapy), it is clear that self-acceptance is the beginning of change.

In the later stages of the group process it is more difficult to put the characteristics into any order. Some elements are:

1. The cracking of facades (members find it unbearable that somebody is speaking through a facade).
2. Giving and receiving feedback.
3. The developing of helping relationships outside the group sessions.
4. The expression of positive feelings and closeness (Devonshire, 1991: 21–23).

The facilitator's job is not, therefore, to direct the group, suggest that it explores feelings or ideas in any particular way, or to interpret individual or group behaviour. The group is trusted to find its own direction, and to work in whatever ways group members find comfortable. In Rogers' view, facilitators should not introduce procedures or structured experiences into encounter groups, but he was not against games and exercises *per se*:

> I try to avoid any procedure that is planned ... If any planned procedure is tried, the group members should be as fully in on it as the facilitator, and should make the choice themselves as to whether they want to use that approach ... To me, nothing is a 'gimmick' if it occurs with real spontaneity. Thus, one may use role playing, bodily contact, psychodrama ... and various other procedures when they seem to express what one is actually feeling at the time (Rogers, 1970).

Coghlan and McIlduff (1990) think that Rogers was more concerned about how structured experiences are employed and from where they originate – from among the participants of the group, or from the facilitator? Offering some structure, is not the same thing as taking control:

> What is important in the person centred approach is how clients or groups may perceive themselves to be controlled or not controlled. Therefore, delicate and subtle structuring, which helps generate spontaneous insights and new learnings that are relevant to client or group needs, is a central point at issue. If structures are offered in a manner that provides freedom for groups to accept or reject them – indeed, to propose other structures – then groups can begin to empower themselves in initiating and implementing their own ways of achieving their purposes (p. 28).

Two Case Studies

Although the general pattern of the development of each group is similar to the description summarised above, groups differ substantially, as the two cases studies that follow demonstrate.

Case Study 1

In 1992 a workshop took place in Greece consisting of young Danish and Greek adults preparing for work experience abroad. The workshop, which was organised by Polly Iossifides and her colleagues of the Person Centred Approach Institute (Hellas), was designed to help the young people develop better communication skills, to explore issues of interpersonal communication across cultural boundaries, and to develop greater levels of self-awareness. The week long workshop did not consist only of encounter groups (there were also some more structured sessions, trips to places of historical interest etc.), but much of the time was spent in groups where the 'agenda' was to explore the personal feelings and relationships that developed among the participants.

In an evaluation of the workshop (Fairhurst and Merry, 1993) the young people were asked to comment on how the week had affected them in different ways. Some comments were:

1. About Personal Awareness and Change

I became more friendly, more tolerant and more hospitable.
I am more in a position to understand without judging other cultures.
These days I trusted some men and I feel really good about it.
I feel less nervous meeting new people in new situations.

2. About the Development of Communication Skills

I learned to listen in a better way to what people tell me without trying to give a solution, but maybe just sharing an experience of mine.
I learned to understand more deeply the others in a psychological sense.
I found ways of communicating I did not know.

3. About Cultural Issues

I can listen to others without prejudice if I try to.
I can accept others and their views more easily.
The most important thing I learned was that we can have relationships regardless of differences.
... I understand better other civilisations without being so condemning and prejudiced.

As all Greeks are not copies of a special model, the same applies to the Danes. So I cannot judge them as mere copies.

4. About the Staff

I was treated in the best possible way – it could not have been better.
We were listened to very carefully, regardless of what we said.
Treated with understanding and respect, love and interest.

A significant fact about this workshop was that it consisted of young people with little or no knowledge of psychology in general, and none of person centred psychology in particular. These were not people training to be counsellors or some other kind of helper, and so they came to the workshop with little knowledge about what it would be like or what was expected of them. What they discovered was a place of psychological safety where the sharing of personal feelings and thoughts became more and more possible as the week went by. The fact that the staff were able to 'model' the qualities of empathic listening, authenticity, respect and non-judgementalism clearly played an important part in the process. The participants felt heard and taken seriously, and, as a result, were able to look again at their ideas and constructs about themselves and others and re-evaluate them.

Case Study 2

This group took place in the Netherlands, meeting once a week for two hours at a time from May 1988 to June 1990. Organised by the South African Community and Culture Centre in Amsterdam, the purpose of the group was to 'provide interested black and white South African exiles with the opportunity to encounter each other on a person-to-person level within an honest and non-coercive environment' (Saley and Holdstock, 1993: 203).

All the group members, which numbered on average about twelve people at each meeting, were resident in the Netherlands. They included authors, actors, teachers, students, a builder and a clerk. There were only two women and fewer black than white members. The white members had left South Africa as conscientious objectors resisting compulsory conscription, or deserting from the South African army. The black members were either escaping from the violence or avoiding imprisonment.

As you might expect, the themes for this group, apart from those connected with the experience of being in exile, also included the political situation in South Africa and the personal relationships between the black and white members of the group. From Saley and

Holdstock's account, it is possible to trace some of the development of this group consistent with the description given above. At first, discussion in the group 'centred around black–white relationships within the community in Amsterdam'. Also, in the early sessions, 'the black participants recounted stories about growing up in black townships, and how they perceived "the other side"'. In other words, discussion was about things external to the group, although obviously very much part of the history and culture the participants brought with them.

After five months or so, however, 'there was a marked change in the frequency and level of self-disclosure in the group'. This self-disclosure was confined mainly to the white members of the group. Saley and Holdstock observe that, 'the main contribution of the black members at this stage was their continuing presence in the group. This presence implied "acceptance" and in a way facilitated the "mourning of the past"'.

The success of this group, as reported by Saley and Holdstock, was its ability to overcome obstacles preventing intimacy and self-disclosure against a background of fear of political persecution among South African refugees. One of the white group members said:

> The experience of the first moments of being personal, and at the same time sharing the nature of others, was profound and delicate at the same time. By profound, I mean real; by delicate, I mean human, a moment for the heart to know (p. 214).

Outcomes

Objective evidence from research studies on positive and negative outcomes of person centred groups is hard to find, perhaps because of the difficulties in conducting meaningful research with small groups that may only meet a few times. Reviews of research studies, however, show some common ways that people change through being in encounter groups. Smith (1975, 1980), for example, found that people feel more positively about themselves, become more open to new experiences, emphasise the giving and receiving of affection, and change in their behaviour (according to observers) by being better communicators and showing more warmth.

A study by Lieberman et al. (1973) suggests that general characteristics of successful encounter groups include the presence of an empathic facilitator, and that structured exercises and games have no lasting positive effects. This study also found a quite high 'casualty rate' among participants. They defined a casualty as someone who experienced an enduring severe negative outcome as a result of participation in one of the groups in the study, e.g. periods of anxiety, depression and, in one case, a manic psychosis. The Lieberman et al. figures were that 7.8% of those starting the group, and 9.1% of those completing over half the group became casualties. This study, however, did attract some criticism. Rowan (1975), for example, criticised the research on the grounds that 'the sample was badly chosen, the assignment to conditions was inappropriate, the psychological environment was ignored (but in fact played a very large part), the measures used were often inappropriate because the relevant work of others in the field was ignored; and hence many of the stated conclusions do not follow from the evidence given' (p. 27). It is also worth noting that the Lieberman et al. research was not a study of person centred encounter groups, but of a whole range of groups of different styles. Only one of the 17 groups included in the study was described as a 'Rogerian marathon'. Others were described as gestalt groups, psychodrama groups or psychoanalytic groups, for example.

The two case studies (above), and the Smith (1975, 1980) studies indicate that at least some encounter group participants report significant positive outcomes. People have found the atmosphere of mutual self-disclosure, the opportunity to make more intimate contact with other people, and the enhanced levels of self-acceptance that can result helpful. In this vein, Brian Thorne (1992) concludes:

> ... I am well aware of the transforming effect such groups can have on many participants. There is a sense in which these experiences can lead to a greatly heightened sense of awareness and a much enhanced feeling both of self-worth and of interconnectedness with others (p. 103).

Criticisms of Encounter

A recent review of encounter groups (Friedman, 1992) echoes previous criticisms of such groups – that they dangerously over-emphasise feeling and its expression at the expense of thinking. Friedman argues that people can be as cut off from the feelings of others as they are from their own, and 'they are programmed to listen for cues and to put other people on pegs rather than really to hear them' (p. 22). Not only do they miss the feelings of others, they also 'miss the plain meaning of what one says ... the very words one utters' (p. 22). Friedman believes that 'in trying to cure this condition people not only turn *to* feelings but *away* from words. The danger of this emphasis on feeling *at the expense of thought* is that we may cease to struggle for the word and take it seriously' (pp. 22–3).

On a different tack, Coulson (1972) has argued that encounter groups did, at one time, offer a chance for people to come together without unrealistic expectations of each other in an environment where mistakes in relating to others could be resolved. He saw the main strength of encounter groups as opportunities for people to relate person-to-person, rather than as representatives of roles or functions. However, he saw dangers in the encounter group becoming institutionalised with rules, procedures, formulas, gurus and credentials. He remarked, 'To be frank, encounter groups are now drowning in gimmickry.'

My Position

I agree very much with Thorne's remarks. As a participant in many encounter groups I have experienced many moments of heightened awareness of myself as a person, and of myself in relationship with others. I have written in more detail elsewhere (Merry and Lusty, 1993) about a particular incident that occurred in an encounter group which concerned the way I thought and felt about myself as a father of two young children, but I can recall many others. Without dismissing the criticisms of Friedman and others, my overwhelming impression of encounter groups is that people do find ways of relating to each other that do away with many, if not all, of the pretences and defences that characterise so much 'ordinary' contact with people. I think there is some merit in Friedman's specific criticism that 'people turn not only to feelings but away from words', but in my experience this is not a common characteristic of person centred groups where thoughts and ideas are as valued as feelings.

Similarly, I do not recognise Coulson's description of encounter groups as in any way typical of person centred groups. I particularly appreciate the person centred style of encounter group with its freedom from games, exercises and other 'structured experiences' imposed by a group leader. I find this approach to be very congruent with the person centred philosophy of trust in people's capacity to find their own direction.

Chapter 17
Can Understanding Lead to Peace?

In the last decade or so there have been enormous political changes. The break-up of the former Soviet Union, the demolishing of the Berlin Wall, and the war in former Yugoslavia contain mixed messages about the possibilities for worldwide peace. South Africa has gone through a revolution with the dismantling of apartheid and the election of Nelson Mandela, the first South African black president. A few years ago, we would not have believed it possible to see members of Palestinian and Israeli political organisations seated round the table discussing ways of bringing peace to the region. Even in Northern Ireland, the political situation is showing some signs of change.

It was in the context of this rapidly changing world that Carl Rogers asked himself how he might contribute to the international peace process, and this chapter takes us full circle in our journey through person centred psychology. We began with discussions about human nature, what motivates us and why and how person centred psychology sees human beings as constructive and social. To put person centred ideas and philosophy to the test in a much larger, political context is a risky undertaking. If the PCA can be shown to be effective in real situations where there is open hostility and aggression, then Rogers' position is strengthened. If, on the other hand, the PCA is shown to be ineffective, or hopelessly optimistic and naive, then Rogers' position is deeply undermined at least in its application outside of the therapy room.

In this chapter I explore how the process of growth and development for individual clients in counselling is similar to the process that occurs in groups when the aim is to work towards the resolution of conflict. In particular, I discuss the concept of *personal power* and, drawing on the ideas of Peggy Natiello (1987, 1990), show how personal power can be extended to a person centred concept of *collaborative power*. Finally, I give some case studies of person centred efforts to confront and explore situations of hostility and conflict.

From Individual to Community

The application of person centred psychology to the exploration of conflict among hostile groups seems, at first sight, a long way from the safe boundaries of individual therapy. This by definition, involves two people only and the focus of the relationship between them is on the inner experiencing of one, the client. Conflict, in this situation, is experienced as largely 'internal'. It may involve conflicts between the person who has been shaped by his or her environment, and the 'real' person underneath who has become alienated from his or her organismic self. It is possible to dislike parts of yourself, and to experience a feeling of being 'at war' with yourself. Of course, it is also possible, and often realistic, for people to feel they are under threat from a hostile environment. As we saw in Chapter 15, for some people the culture is antagonistic to their way of life or convictions and, while counselling may help in coping with hostility, it cannot resolve the problems that exist in the world outside.

In individual counselling a major goal is to reach a deeper understanding of yourself, not necessarily of others. Being more aware of your conditions of worth, and developing more self-acceptance and self-esteem, can help you understand those who appear hostile to you, but it may not directly help you resolve the conflicts that exist between you. However, in person centred psychology there are three principles that modify this position.

First, there is the idea I touched on earlier – that what is most personal is most general (Rogers, 1961: 26). The further we can go in exploring our own processes, and the more we can accept and understand ourselves, the more likely we are to find that what is most true for us also applies to others.

Second, person centred theory argues that the closer an individual comes to Rogers' concept of the 'fully functioning person' the more that individual is likely to value (and be better at) constructive relationships. Furthermore, people who have significantly resolved their conditions of worth are likely to behave in increasingly socially constructive ways. The fully functioning person is more open to and accepting of the experiences of others, and is less dogmatic about 'right' and 'wrong'.

Third, is the concept of *personal power*. Natiello (1987) describes this as 'the ability to act effectively under one's own volition rather than under external control ... the individual is aware of and can act upon his or her own feelings, needs, and values rather than looking to others for direction' (p. 210). In individual counselling, it is this shift in the locus of evaluation – from external to internal – that is often characteristic of the process. Natiello (1990) went on to distinguish the kind of personal power, or autonomy, that involves independence and separation from others, from that which 'involves reciprocity of feeling, blended with a recognition of the separateness of others' (p. 275), to make possible what she terms 'collaborative power':

> It is in the recognition of interrelatedness, the regard for others' needs and feelings, the understanding that what affects one of us affects all of us, that collaborative power becomes possible (p. 275).

The combination of these three things, (1) the generality of human experience that makes deep understanding of others possible, (2) the tendency towards constructive social relationships and action of the fully functioning person, and (3) the realisation that personal power can be translated into collaborative power, underpin the person centred approach to conflict exploration and the search for peace among antagonistic groups.

Collaborative Power

Natiello (1990) contrasts collaborative power with traditional authoritarian power. Relationships that develop in a society with an authoritarian power system 'are characterised by domination and subordination; they promote competition over cooperation; and they are costly to those who hold the power as well as to those over whom it is held' (p. 269). Collaborative power, by contrast, 'relies on caring about others' needs as well as one's own and on respect for and belief in the ability of individuals to strive for the common good' (p. 272).

Natiello (1990) identifies five obstacles to the creation of collaborative power in groups:

1. People have become used to, and expect, certain behaviour from group leaders. When the leader, or facilitator, fails to lead in an authoritarian manner, people can become frustrated and disenchanted.
2. There is a belief that there is not enough power to go round, and that some people have it, while others do not. When a person centred facilitator fails to exert power, somebody else will. Groups need time to build trust that there is sufficient power for everyone.
3. People who have learned to be subordinate can become fearful when facilitative leaders do not exercise power in the way they have come to expect from authoritarian leaders.
4. Power is widely believed to be coercive and exploitive, and this can dissuade some people from claiming any power at all, including their personal power. 'Collaborative systems depend on open, full participation of each member. Persons who hold themselves back out of fear of 'taking over' often impede the success of the experience' (p. 282).
5. A community of collaborative power requires different ways of

thinking and behaving from the way people generally have become accustomed. It can be difficult to give up familiar ways of being and try something new and, at first, threatening.

Natiello (1990) also believes that there are some obstacles that have to be overcome by person centred facilitators if they are to be effective in groups. They are, firstly, a tendency to put their own needs in the group to one side to the extent that they appear to participants to be 'untouchable and invulnerable' (p. 278). In such situations, facilitators can be perceived as guru-like, and hence retain power without making it available to the group. In a similar fashion, a facilitator who fails to self-disclose at all can reproduce the hierarchical power model. '... I believe that lack of self-disclosure in a relationship results in the kind of power imbalance that characterises dominant–subordinate relationships. Thus, withholding information can lead to a power-over position' (pp. 278–9). Fourth, a facilitator who does not accept fully the concept that the actualising tendency can be relied on to operate in a group as much as in an individual client, might be tempted to take over when the group appears disturbed or chaotic. Finally, facilitators need to be clear and genuine about their intentions. Interventions that are designed to redirect the group, however subtly, are unlikely to encourage a collaborative atmosphere.

Although Natiello identifies these difficulties in the process of developing collaborative power in groups, she is certain that where it can be done there are very creative outcomes:

> It is revolutionary in that it removes the political value of authoritarian power from its primary position and replaces it with a vision of collaborative power that is characterized by nurturance and growth. The result of such a shift in political structure is a metamorphosis in values. Interdependence, caring, compassion, cooperation, and nonviolence replace the fierce independence, dominance, competition, and potential violence ... that characterize the prevailing authoritarian structure (p. 284).

I would add one further potential obstacle to the development of a collaborative power system, especially where the group concerned consists of people from more than one culture. Bearing in mind the discussion in Chapter 15, it is crucial that facilitators understand the varying cultural expectations that may be present within the group (as well as the other issues discussed in that chapter). What may appear to be 'democratic' in one culture, for instance, may well be viewed with suspicion by another. An example will help illustrate this.

One group, held in Szeged, Hungary, in 1986, consisted of upwards of two hundred people. The group had met together to explore issues of cross-cultural communication within a person centred framework. The group consisted of many nationalities, including Hungarian, British, American, Irish, French, German, Italian, Czechoslovakian and other Europeans. Early in the group's life, there was a discussion about how much time to spend together as a large community, and how much to spend in smaller groups. Western European and North American participants wanted the decision taken 'democratically', i.e. by vote, but this was being resisted by the people from Eastern Europe. As a facilitator, I did not know how to contribute to the resolution of this problem. I had naively failed to understand that on a subjective level democracy is experienced very differently in Eastern Europe from Western Europe and the USA. The Eastern Europeans were clearly looking for an experience different from the political system under which they lived their daily lives, but were not prepared to have 'Western' ideas of democracy forced on them.

A related issue concerns the extent to which facilitators are 'culturally self-aware' (Ridley et al., 1994). In the context of the present discussion this involves the extent to which facilitators are aware of their own cultural inheritance, and how historically their culture has impinged on the culture of others. An illustration of this occurred during 1985 when I facilitated an encounter group in a workshop in Dublin. A Southern Irish woman expressed her resentment to me as an English man (the only one in the room) for the way the English had forced her to abandon her mother tongue – the Irish language. Her remark was, 'You have stolen the language of my heart'.

This workshop of about two hundred people provided a good example of a person centred approach to exploring personal and political issues in large groups. Immediately after it I wrote some notes that capture some of what I experienced, and I hope the following extract gives a flavour of it.

A Workshop in Cross-cultural Communication – Dublin, 1985

This workshop was one of a series of similar events held annually for more than twenty years, organised by Charles Devonshire, Director of the Centre for Cross-Cultural Communication. They are attempts to provide a person centred environment in which people can come together to explore the problems and issues in understanding and communicating with each other across cultural and linguistic boundaries:

> One of the most impressive aspects of the week for me was the fact that when people are determined to communicate, they will do so even against enormous odds. The large group met together for at least three hours every day, breaking into smaller encounter or option groups for the remainder of the time. It was at one of the large group meetings that the passionate issue of the situation in Northern Ireland arose. For almost three hours the vari-

ous groups involved – Northern Ireland Catholics and Protestants, Southern Irish and English – expressed their political and personal feelings. It was a stormy time with a lot of rage and even verbal violence. After a while, though, because the group had worked hard to produce a climate in which people were listened to and respected as individuals, there seemed to emerge the beginnings of understanding and acceptance between people. I am not claiming that anything was finally resolved, but people did have the real experience that where communication is facilitated people are often able to appreciate the 'humanness' of the other side, and this to me is very hopeful. A broader aspect of this exchange was that because it was so centrally concerned with issues of power and control, other groups present could relate their own feelings and experiences. When it comes to issues such as these, many people have something to say, including South Americans, Poles and Hungarians.

Three Case Studies in Conflict Exploration

Rogers (1977: 122) described his view of conflict among both individuals and groups in straightforward terms, '*Each* of the parties involved holds with equal conviction, an identical view: "I am right and you are wrong; I am good and you are bad."'

The simple language in which this idea is expressed, however, does not do full justice to the complexities that are involved in situations where people find themselves in conflict with one another. People sometimes commit hostile or aggressive acts against others even when they know it is wrong to do so. They are not defending a particular right, or a rational idea of 'goodness', and they do not perceive the victims of their acts as either wrong or bad. Although such simple ideas can be offered as motives for hostile acts, the truth usually turns out to be more involved and complex. The three examples that follow are of extremely complicated political situations, and space does not allow for a detailed examination of all those complexities. I think the examples do show, however, that Rogers and his colleagues were aware of most, if not all, the complexities involved and tried to understand and incorporate them into their way of working.

Northern Ireland

This involved an encounter group held with ten participants; four Catholics, five Protestants and a retired English Army Colonel. Participants, both men and women, represented moderate and extremist views. In Rogers' words, 'In the early sessions the bitterness, horror and despair of everyday life in Belfast was abundantly clear' (Rogers, 1978: 130).

One participant's sister had been killed by a bomb, another had several times been at the aftermath of bombings, and another's son had been on the receiving end of British Army patrols' behaviour, on one occasion believing he was about to be shot. During the group a Protestant participant said, 'If I seen an IRA man lying on the ground – this is the wrong thing I suppose in your eyes – I would *step* on him, because to me he has just went out and taken the lives of innocent people.'

In the group meetings, a great deal of hatred, mistrust and suspicion was expressed and, 'The individuals were speaking not only for themselves but for generations of resentment and prejudice' (p. 131). Although the group only met for sixteen hours, in Rogers' estimation 'centuries-old hatreds were not only softened but in some instances deeply changed' (p. 131).

This group was filmed, although some parts of the film were deleted because it was felt their inclusion might endanger the lives of some of the participants. After the encounter group ended, some participants continued to meet and formed teams of two – one Protestant and one Catholic – showing the film to Church groups and leading discussions.

This example (and the two that follow) are best seen as contained, 'laboratory' situations in which the principles of the person centred approach are being tested. While Rogers does report some positive outcomes from the Belfast group, its impact on the wider political scene is obviously limited. Rogers does not tell us how the group was selected, or how much direct involvement (if any) any of the participants had in the 'troubles' in Northern Ireland. There has been no follow-up research to determine whether changes in attitudes were permanent, or a temporary result of the intensive 'group effect'.

South Africa

Carl Rogers (with his colleague, Ruth Sanford) first visited South Africa in the summer of 1982. They had been invited to a multi-racial conference in Johannesburg, attended by 600 people, and as part of this conference offered to facilitate a small multiracial encounter group on stage. Unsurprisingly perhaps, the first volunteers for this group were white men and women. At first, only one black woman came forward. Eventually, however, eleven participants of the conference volunteered to take part in the group – four white men (Steve, Colin, Alan and Jeff), three white women (Shirley, Stephanie and Rhoda), two black men (John and Edward), and two black women (Daphne and Jane).

Sanford (1991a) has provided a transcript of the dialogue that took place. I have selected parts of it here, mindful of the fact that my selection may be unrepresentative of the event as a whole. We focus on the experience of Daphne, one of the black women in the group, rather than try and follow all the themes and issues that emerged. There is, as you would expect, some discussion of the general political situation in

South Africa, and there are examples given of how black people were constantly reminded of their politically inferior status. But there are also examples of both black and white participants gradually reaching out to each other in more direct and personal ways.

Towards the beginning of the group, Colin is talking about the progress towards political change, but that it cannot happen overnight. He talks about the reluctance of whites to give up their political power, and that this reluctance is based on fear: *'We're reluctant to give up for fear of reprisals and when we give it up we're a minority and we'll lose out, we'll be exposed to discomfort, our lives endangered, our economy will go down. Even as I like my position of privilege, I know it is wrong.'*

In response, John (a black member of the group) raises his voice and speaks with some anger: *'You speak about those in power. You have voted them into power and they've been in power plenty long enough to be of no use to anybody!'*

Daphne, feels differently: *'I'm tired of such talks. I feel very confident sitting here and I don't feel I am sitting with whites. I'm in this group and this group has people'.* Daphne goes on to describe how her most urgent concern is that her children grow up feeling good about themselves as black people, and that *'they be strong within themselves.'*

A little later, Steve responds to Daphne, saying he appreciates her point of view but that if he were black, he would be feeling a lot of anger. Daphne replies, *'Mistake me not! If you ask what is my basic attitude towards whites, I am very angry. And I'm bitter that whites have given me an unnecessary job of building my child's positive self-image.'* She tells how she finds her daughter cutting white pictures from magazines, *'And I am angry having to say, "Ntlanta, I think here are some beautiful black pictures. Look at this one. This one is black. Not everything that matters is white".'*

Anger and fear are two very present emotions in this group. Daphne expresses some of it beautifully when she says, *'For me it started like you as a white man gained the upper hand over me personally. But I am at the stage where sometimes I look at whites I feel very sorry for them. Very sorry that they are gripped in fear. And sometimes I gloat over it. Because I look at them and say, 'God, how scared you are! Let them be scared!' Because they wasted so much fearing to reach out to me as a person. Like Edward, I've discovered that you can reach a place where you can relate to a white man and say, 'My God, there are whites who can be downright human, who can look at you as a human being. But whites being scared, I say it's your problem.'*

Daphne later continues with her feeling that she wants to relate to individual people in the group, not people as representative of whites or blacks, *'When you talk about masses I feel that there is nothing we can do, because I can never change the attitudes of whites. But I can change Alan's attitude and I think he can also change mine.'*

A little later, Daphne says, *'The other thing about reaching out is that it's painful. You've got to take the risks that go with it. I've had to go through that pain. It's not easy.'*

A little further on, Rhoda tells how difficult it is for her to reach out to black people, *'I'm scared to get involved with you because I'm scared you're going to blame me and hit out at me as a person, for where you're at. And yeah, I'm afraid.'*

Carl Rogers observes that when the talk is in general terms, *'then the feelings are deeply opposed; that's when the feelings of bitterness and hatred come out. When we speak of person-to-person contacts, then the tone becomes quite different. The feeling is very different. That is a very significant aspect of our discussion.'*

Shortly after this, when Daphne has returned to the theme of 'reaching out', Alan reaches out to touch Daphne's hand, but Daphne slaps the hand away. She tells Alan he is making her feel not a member of the group. She doesn't know why Alan is reaching out to her in this way: *'... I don't know whether you are reaching out to me because you are saying, "Here is Daphne, she's a black woman and she's expressing such nice views about blackness." And give me the feeling of being singled out. If you can hold my hand, you can hold Jane's and John's.'*

At one point, Carl Rogers asks Daphne, *'Did you feel you were being patted on the back?'* But Daphne is not sure what to say, except she feels it has something to do with Alan as a person, not Alan as a white person.

The group ends shortly after Daphne makes a statement to the audience who, from time to time had called things out or applauded, *'I felt bad that when Jeff, in particular, made comments that he had to get some counter-reactions from the audience, because basically I do not feel that was helpful. I really prefer to sit down with a white man who can be white in his own way as Jeff was. I wanted to say to those in the audience who interrupted, Please give Jeff a chance to be himself. It's only interacting with people like Jeff that you can find a way to react with him.'*

Jeff reaches over to Daphne and holds out his hand, and she accepts it. Jeff says, *'That makes me feel good. You've accepted me as a person and I feel I can accept you as a person. It's tremendous.'*

Rogers and Sanford returned to South Africa in 1986 and continued their work. Reflecting on her experiences both then and in 1982, Sanford (1991b) wrote:

Increasingly we have the conviction that most major changes are precipitated by a great stress or crisis; that a person and perhaps a nation, pushed to the brink of disaster can respond by panic and disintegration, by violence against others or themselves, or by openness to the pain and the risk of accepting change. Only through this third alternative can healing and renewal begin. It is this alternative which we have shown is possible (pp. 89–90).

Ruth Sanford's concluding thoughts are worth giving here for their optimistic and, as it turned out, prophetic nature:

> It is my opinion that President de Klerk and Nelson Mandela can lead the way to the more hopeful and positive solution to the great South African dilemma. This does not mean that pain, suffering, conflict, sacrifice and even dying for many can be avoided. But it means that if leaders on opposite sides can listen to one another in good faith, commit themselves to a positive relationship, differ from, but have respect for each other, express their feelings and opinions openly, there is hope (p. 90).

Central America

In 1985 Rogers and a group of his colleagues were involved in organising and participating in a workshop on the theme of 'The Central American Challenge' (Rogers, 1986c). It took place in a hotel in Rust, Austria, and there were several unusual features to this event. Firstly, it consisted of fifty participants drawn from influential political, academic and other institutional contexts. For example, there were three ex-presidents of Central American countries, the current vice-president of Costa Rica, a number from ministries of foreign affairs, seven ambassadors, university professors, peace activists and writers. Second, the workshop was not a media event, but a private gathering in which the participants were encouraged to meet as persons rather than as political or representative figures. Third, the workshop was facilitated by a group of staff experienced in person centred ways of exploring conflict.

According to Rogers (1986c) there were four main purposes to the workshop: (1) to bring together influential individuals involved in international relations, particularly those concerning Central America; (2) to offer the experience of a staff group committed to facilitating person-to-person encounters; (3) to facilitate free expression among the participants to encourage understanding, reduce tension and enhance communication; (4) to help establish greater trust that would, in turn, create initiatives leading to more peaceful relationships between nations.

In Rogers' words, 'The workshop had more significance, more impact, opened more lines of communication, brought together more divergent persons than we had any reasonable right to expect' (p. 24).

The workshop was not without its problems. For example, the translators made the staff aware that because of their cultural differences, the staff inadvertently offended members of other cultures. It also seemed that the facilitative staff separated themselves from the participants too much, and probably were seen as aloof by some. Nevertheless, in Rogers' estimation this workshop was a success partly, for example, because its private nature enabled participants to speak frankly and 'off the record', and partly because the staff group were experienced in facilitating communication in situations of potential (and actual) conflict.

Another element that contributed to the success of this workshop was the coincidental happening of the *Heurigen*, an ancient Austrian custom celebrating the grape harvest. During the festivities, the participants were able to relax and enjoy themselves together, fortified by quantities of the season's new wine. Informal events such as this are often underestimated in their importance to the development of trust and good relationships among group members. It seemed certain to Rogers that the *Heurigen* provided an excellent atmosphere, and an opportunity for relationships to be formed and deepened.

Rogers measured the success of the workshop in terms of the personal relationships that were established among members of the group, and the extent to which mistrust and hostility were gradually replaced by a more trusting and open atmosphere. As with the South African example, there were periods in which hostility and anger were openly expressed. Gradually, however, these attitudes gave way to a greater willingness to hear and understand opposing points of view and a belief that reconciliation was achievable.

Some Concluding Comments

While single events like the ones described above do not, in themselves, have much impact on the international political scene, they do provide practical evidence that conflicts can be handled effectively employing a person centred approach. Rogers was not, however, interested only in providing evidence and perspectives, but in making a practical difference that could be built on by others. His work took him to many countries, among them Japan, Mexico, Venezuela, Brazil, Hungary, Poland, South Africa and the Soviet Union. In all of these places he was concerned with individual experience and meaning, but he tried always to see personal experience in its social, cultural and political context.

His belief, and the theoretical ideas he developed, led him to approach people, even hostile and angry people, with a confidence that if he could really hear those people, and help others to hear them, the outcome would be individually and socially constructive. The research he undertook into conflict exploration was not objective; he involved himself deeply in the process – a kind of action research. The evidence that he provided is not statistically valid, but it was not meant

to be. The general influence of this kind of 'evidence' is difficult to esti-
mate, but there is little doubt that person centred ideas have touched
and encouraged thousands of people.

The essence of Rogers' life and work was a theoretical belief in the
value of effective communication, and a continuing search for means of
putting that belief into practice, at first with individuals, then with
groups and finally with whole communities. Carl Rogers died at the age
of 85 shortly after being nominated for the Nobel Peace Prize.

Appendix
An Interview Between Carl
Rogers and Ms G.

Carl: OK? ... I don't know what you might like to talk about but I'd be very willing to listen.

Ms G.: (Pause) I'm just at the moment feeling how afraid I am of talking to you.

Carl: Frightened of me, or frightened of the situation, or both?

Ms G.: In a way it's both 'cos ... it's like ... me being in this situation am I forced to, and I mean when like I say 'forced' I don't mean externally, I mean forced in a way to meet with you and also to meet with myself.

Carl: So you have to make yourself ... come forward to meet.

Ms G.: Yeh, and I'm just thinking about how much I avoid doing that. I feel OK about meeting people and ... spending a little bit of time with them ... but there's always a point where I want to run away and I think a lot of the time I do ... when it feels like it's getting too close.

Carl: So you like to go a little ways in meeting them but there's some point when you feel 'No ... now we would *really* meet if we went any further' and you'd like to run away.

Ms G.: Yes ... and ... I'm thinking that it's funny it's. I'm not afraid of what it is in *you* ... I'm afraid of what's in *me* and, it's like in a way that I can con myself about what's in me if I don't meet with you, if I meet with you I have to give you something of me.

Carl: So the block is not in me, it's that if you go *too* far you'll reveal something of *you*.
(Pause)

Ms G.: I ... er ... For a long time I've felt like there, there is this *thing* in *me* and I don't know what it is ... and ... sometimes when I hear other people talking I ... and it's not so much the words that they're using but the feelings that I can sense in them ... of ... um ... I feel heavy and I know that their feelings are touching the same kind of feelings in me.

Carl: They're touching that secret part of you that you don't quite know what it is.

Ms G.: Mm a lot of the time that is hurt or pain and sometimes it's anger as well.

Carl: But you feel that whatever this is that is sort of frightening within, is of negative feelings of pain and hurt and possibly anger.

Ms G.: (Nods) And if I get in touch with them that they will overwhelm me and there's a fear of getting lost in them somehow and of not being able to find my way back to the joy that I can feel.

Carl: That if you ever let yourself really live in or feel those feelings. Maybe you'd never find your way back to pleasantness and happiness and joy.

Ms G.: 'Cos I feel like I *can't* let go of things like hurt and I can't let go of things like resentment ... I *want* to, I *want* to let go of those things, but I don't know how, how to do that, so I don't want to explore them, I feel that if I explore them they will always be with me and I've kind of learnt to experience joy ... but having said that to you I'm questioning whether that joy is real.

Carl: Makes you wonder whether maybe the joy would be more real if you were able to explore some of those frightening feelings.

Ms G.: (Nods) (Pause)

Carl: But they are scary.

Ms G.: And I've put them away for such a long time it seems like ...

Carl: Resentment and hurt and everything like that have just kept and pushed down for a long, long time.

Ms G.: And there's this rational part of me that says that I don't have a right to feel those things and that I can understand the reasons why the hurt is there and that I should care for the other person that gave me that hurt and it's like in caring for the other person I kind of have to hide the hurt that they've caused me.

Carl: So you kind of talk it all away and explain why you shouldn't really feel those feelings are not necessary ... and you shouldn't feel them in relation to the person who caused them.

Ms G.: Um ... (Laughs) ... I've just realised while you were feeding that back that I *know* the person who caused them, or ... (Pause) ... hah ... I feel a bit funny about saying 'caused' ... I know how much ... I think I'm doing it again, I'm taking away everything from the other person and saying that they didn't cause it ... *I'm* the cause ... I was just about to rationalise that I'm the person who caused it and that they couldn't possibly have caused it.

Carl: Certainly, you can't feel any blame for that person ... it must be you ... and yet somehow you know you *do* feel that resentment and hurt.

Ms G.: (Nodding)

Carl: ... and you know the person that it's directed toward.
(Pause)

Ms G.: I feel like I have to put myself in a box that ... (Pause) ... I *do*, I *do* feel the resentment but I don't *want* to because ... how do you get rid of the feelings and ...like that? ... and I don't want to live those feelings.

Carl: It's safer to keep it in a box and yet you know very well that you *feel* it and you're scared ... *if* you feel it, then what? Will you ever get rid of it?

Ms G.: (Nods) ... (Long pause) ... I'd like to tell you the person I feel this for, and it's ... actually it's not just one person it's my parents, my mother and my father, but it's more with my mother because she's, I don't know ... I feel it more or it's awakened more in me with my mother because she's around and my father isn't. (Pause) ... And ... I kind of feel like ... I was going to say 'they' ... I, like trapped myself in the past, somehow, but things that I feel angry about ... from way back ... and I'm still stuck there and I can't move on until I've dealt with it, but I don't know how to do that.

Carl: So you know it's your mother mostly, and you know the feelings that were stirred up a long time ago, but how you can work through those, that you're not quite clear.

Ms G.: (Nods) ... (Pause) ... And now that causes me to ... er ... not be me ... I, I think about things I said to my mother like 'I love you and I understand why those things happened' and things like that, but I've never been able to show her how hurt I feel about it all.

Carl: Again you can explain it away that there are reasons and so on, it's OK, but you've never been able to let her see the hurt and pain that is in *you* ... and somehow that keeps you from *being* all of you.

Ms G.: I feel like I have to protect her somehow.

Carl: Mm, you've got to care for *her*.

Ms G.: And so every day I push down the hurt and I push down the anger and I push down the resentment and I just ... and I'm somebody else.

Carl: That your daily task is to push 'em down, push 'em down, push 'em down and be somebody that isn't quite real.

Ms G.: And every day I spend time trying to get in touch with the feelings that I know are there but are so far away, and so I'm stuck in the past thinking 'Oh! I can't relate to this person because I'm afraid of, of these feelings inside me and that's all because of these feelings that happened in the past and if only I could feel the feelings but I can't and ...'

Carl: So you see it all very clearly, but to try to get in touch with, or to express those feelings of hurt and resentment, that's where you ... can't do it. (A few words unintelligible.)

Ms G.: I, er I get rid of little bits of it on other people, you know (laughing) you can do something really simple to me and I can resent it, you know and I enjoy feeling resentful.

Carl: You're feeling you let out a little bit of it even though you exaggerate the situation in order to feel that resentment, and it lets out a little of the resentment from the past.

Ms G.: That's exactly it, I didn't use the word 'exaggeration' but, er, situations occur sometimes and I exaggerate them so that they can fit into this pattern so that I can feel the resentment and ... (Laughs).

Carl: So you're quite ingenious in finding ways of expressing bits of it.

Ms G.: Yeah ... I am ... (Long pause) ... (Sighs and shakes head)

Carl: I wonder what that shaking of your head means ... It looks like you're saying 'Isn't possible'.

Ms G.: I was saying 'Isn't possible' and I was thinking that I can't blame, I can't *blame* it on anybody that ...and I was thinking I can't ... um ... I wanted to tell you a bit about what happened and ... but then I thought that by telling you I'd kind of be blaming it on something and

Carl: It's got to come out so carefully that it doesn't blame anybody or anything, you can't just let it out.

Ms G.: That's what's so awful about it, I know it reminded. ... I'm running this battle somehow with my emotions, but maybe it *is* OK to blame and to say, to get it all out, and then when it's all out maybe I can do something with it that makes it OK with everybody concerned, but ...

Carl: So it's quite possible that it's OK to be unreasonable and irrational even, spill things that aren't quite right, because then you might then be able to make it OK afterwards once they were out.
(Pause)

Ms G.: I just realised something ... part of the hurt is about not being considered and I'm talking about when I was young and my parents kept on getting back together again and separating and getting back together again and separating and I went into children's homes and all sorts of things that I wasn't considered, and now what I'm doing is not considering myself, I'm not ... it's like I can't consider myself, I don't think that I'm important enough to be considered.

Carl: That childhood experience of being shuttled around and not really considered in the situation ... er ... resulted in you not being able to consider and take care of yourself ... (Pause) ... and you must have felt very keenly the business of being treated as an object, just put here, put there and not really, not really considered, not really cared about.

Ms G.: I mean how can you say what you want when you're four?
(Pause)

Carl: How can you possibly say when you're four years old 'Hey! look at me, I need to be considered, I need to be thought about.'

Ms G.: (Weeps)

Carl: I guess you're saying and feeling it now ... (Pause) ... and it hurt like hell.
(Pause)

Ms G.: ...and even now I can't consider myself, I feel like I've got to wipe the tears away and talk to you and ...

Carl: Don't have any undue show of emotion ... got to be polite and proper.

Ms G.: I always feel guilty when I'm crying, you know, I always feel as though I'm not allowed to cry.

Carl: Don't cry ... be a big girl ... but when the tears were dropping that was the 4-year-old feeling very hurt.
(Pause)

Ms G.: And angry, very angry.

Carl: And angry ... (Unintelligible) ... Damn you, why don't you consider me?
(Pause)

Ms G.: (Wipes tears) Now my rational mind has come back and I'm saying I understood how it was with your mother, she's told you a bit about that.

Carl: So don't feel those feelings, there were reasons for your mother's actions ... mustn't feel those feelings.

Ms G.: She'd feel very hurt if I ... It's almost like a reverse ... I feel like her mother sometimes, like I have to reassure her that it's OK.

Carl: You didn't hurt me.

Ms G.: Yeah.

Carl: It's not true, but still you must be a good mother to her.

Ms G.: And that makes me angry sometimes too.

Carl: Why do I have to be *her* mother?

Ms G.: Yeah ... (Pause) ... I'm frightened now that I might get lost in what it is I'm feeling.

Carl: It's scary to let yourself down into those feelings, you might not be able to get out.

Ms G.: But it almost feels like self-pity and I don't know I can accept that, that I pity myself or I feel sorry for myself.

Carl: You almost feel ashamed of that but you do feel sorry for yourself.

Ms G.: (Nods)

Carl: You realise, 'I went through a helluva lot' ... (pause) ... 'I really do feel pity for myself'.

Ms G.: (Laughs) I've washed it away now. I'm thinking about that time when I was in the children's home, it was a Catholic home. It was a convent and they used to say things like that, like you know, everyone's got this thing about pity yourself, that you should think about other people and that was so much around me at that time and I think I really learnt it very well.

Carl: You just don't feel things like that, you think about other people ... it was a good lesson in sitting on your feelings ... You learnt it all too well.

Ms G.: It wasn't such a good lesson, I know that; I feel good because ... I somehow feel I'm just beginning to feel those feelings ... I talked about, they're coming out a little bit at a time.

Carl: It's not quite so frightening because you realise 'Yes, I am able to be in touch with them and they're not overwhelming me, coming out little by little'.
(Long pause)

Ms G. I somehow wish I could explore more with you.

Carl: You wish?

Ms G.: I wish I could explore more with you, because I don't feel frightened with you.

Carl: You feel that this is a fairly safe place, that I'm a fairly safe person to explore them with.

Ms G. Yes.

Carl: You'd like to get at more of it. There's the hurt and anger of being shuttled back and forth and there's the suppression of the convent, the orphanage, but there are others.

Ms G.: (Nods) There's a lot more.

Carl: A lot more.

Ms G.: At the moment I don't feel as frightened as I did, although I'm sure that might come back, that fear.

Carl: But for the moment they don't seem quite so scary.

Ms G.: And that feels like such a relief because, I was just thinking about all the times that I meet people and the fear is there, and how much it stops me from being with people sometimes.

Carl: It's really good to have that fear lessened a little when it's really stopped you from some (Unintelligible).
(Pause)

Ms G.: And I think I'm also getting the feeling that what's so bad about telling other people that I'm hurt?

Carl: What's the big deal, what's the big crime in saying I'm hurt, I am hurting. Why does that seem so bad?

Ms G.: And it has.
(Pause)

Ms G.: I think perhaps because I was trying to be somebody else.

Carl: Trying to be someone that you were not.

Ms G.: Trying to be what other people wanted me to be, I think. I think it's all part of them not considering me, and considering other people, what it is that they want from me, how they want me to be.

Carl: So I've got to be what they would like and not consider me.

Ms G.: I think I'll be me for a while.

Carl: You think you'll be *you* for a while did you say?

Ms G.: Yes.

Carl: Might be a good experiment, huh?

Ms G.: Yes.

Carl: You'll really consider yourself and be yourself and not try to be what other people want you to be. (Pause) We're going to have to stop in a couple of minutes ... OK to stop now?

Ms G.: Yes.

Carl: Good.

References

AXLINE, V.M. (1969) *Play Therapy*, revised edition. New York: Ballantine Books.

BAYNE, R., HORTON, I., MERRY, T. AND NOYES, E. (1994) *The Counsellor's Handbook*. London: Chapman and Hall.

BIMROSE, J. (1993) Counselling and social context. In: Bayne, R. and Nicolson, P. (Eds) *Counselling and Psychology for Health Professionals*.London: Chapman and Hall.

BOZARTH, J. (1993) A theoretical reconceptualisation of the necessary and sufficient conditions for therapeutic personality change. *Person-Centred Journal*2(1).

BRODLEY, B. AND BRODY A. (1990) Understanding client-centred therapy through interviews conducted by Carl Rogers. Paper for the panel, *Fifty Years of Client-centred Therapy: Recent Research*. American Psychological Association annual meeting, Boston, MA, USA.

CAMPBELL, D.T. (1967) Stereotypes and the perception of group differences. *American Psychologist* 22, 817–29.

CHAPLIN, J. (1989) Counselling and gender. In: Dryden, W., Charles-Edwards, D. and Woolfe, R. (Eds) *Handbook of Counselling in Britain*.London: Routledge.

COGHLAN, D. AND MCILDUFF, E. (1990) Structuring and nondirectiveness in group facilitation. *Person-Centred Review* 5(1), 13–29.

COULSON, W.R. (1972) *Groups, Gimmicks and Instant Gurus*. New York: Harper & Row.

COURT, G. (1987) *Of Primary Importance*. Published by The Tower Hamlets Primary Teacher Support Group.

D'ARDENNE, P. AND MAHTANI, A. (1989) *Transcultural Counselling in Action*. London: Sage.

DAVIS, C.M. (1928) Self selection of diet by newly weaned infants. *American Journal of Diseases of Children* 36(4), 651–79.

DEVONSHIRE, C. (1991) The person-centred approach and cross-cultural communication. *The Person-Centred Approach and Cross-Cultural Communication* 1, No. 1.

DEWEY, J. (1906) *The School and the Child*. Blackie.

DEWEY, J. (1915) *Democracy and Education*. Macmillan.

EGELAND, B. AND STROUFE, L. (1981) Attachment and early maltreatment. *Child Development* 52, 44–52.

FAIRHURST, I. (1990) *The Village Project – An Evaluation*. Unpublished document, King Alfred School, London.

FAIRHURST, I. AND MERRY, T. (1993) A Greek experience. *Person Centred Practice* 1(2).

FESCHBACH, N.D. AND FESCHBACH, S. (1969) The relationship between empathy and aggression in two age groups. *Developmental Psychology* 1, 102–7.

FIEDLER, F.E. (1950) A comparison of therapeutic relationships in psychoanalytic, non-directive and Adlerian therapy. *Journal of Consulting Psychology* 14, 436–45.

FRIEDMAN, M. (1992) *Dialogue and the Human Image*. London: Sage.

GALEF, B.G. (1991) A contrarian view of the wisdom of the body as it relates to dietary self-selection. *Psychological Review* 98(2), 218–23.

GARFORTH, F.W. (Ed.) (1966) *Dewey on Education*. London: Victor Gollancz.

GUTHRIE FORD, J. (1991) Rogers's theory of personality: Review and perspectives. In: Jones, A. and Crandall, R. (Eds) *Handbook of Actualisation, a Special Issue of Journal of Social Behaviour and Personality*. 6(5).

HEMMING, J. (1980) *The Betrayal of Youth*. London: Marion Boyars.

HJELLE, L.A. AND ZIEGLER, D.J. (1981) *Personality Theories*. McGraw Hill.

JOHNSON, D.W., JOHNSON, R.G., MARUYAMA, G., NELSON, D. AND SKON, L. (1981) Effects of cooperative, competitive, and individualistic goals structures on achievement: A meta-analysis. *Psychological Bulletin* 89, 47–62.

KIRSCHENBAUM, H. AND HENDERSON, V. (Eds) (1989a) *The Carl Rogers Reader*. Boston: Houghton Mifflin.

KIRSCHENBAUM, H. AND HENDERSON, V. (Eds) (1989b) *The Carl Rogers Dialogues*. Boston: Houghton Mifflin.

KOHUT, H. (1978) *The Search for the Self. Selected Writings of Heinz Kohut: 1950–1978*, Vol. 1. New York: International Universities Press.

KRASNER, L. (1965) The behaviour scientist and social responsibility: No place to hide. *Journal of Social Issues* 21(2), 9–30.

LAGO, C. AND THOMPSON, J. (1989) Counselling and race. In: Dryden, W., Charles-Edwards, D. and Woolfe, R. (Eds) *Handbook of Counselling in Britain*. London: Tavistock/Routledge.

LAWRENCE, E. (1970) *Origins and Growth of Modern Education*. London: Pelican.

LIEBERMAN, M., YALOM, I. AND MILES, M. (1973) *Encounter Groups: First Facts*. New York: Basic Books.

LLEWELYN, S. AND OSBORN, K. (1983) Women as clients and therapists. In: Pilgrim, D. (Ed.) *Psychology and Psychotherapy: Current Trends and Issues*. London: Routledge.

MASLOW, A. (1971) *The Farther Reaches of Human Nature*. London: Penguin.

MAY, R. (1969) *Love and Will*. New York: Dell Publishing.

MAY, R. (1982) The problem of evil: an open letter to Carl Rogers. *Journal of Humanistic Psychology* 22(3), 10–21.

MCFADDEN, J. (1988) Cross-cultural counselling: Caribbean perspective. *Journal of Multicultural Counseling and Development* 16, 36–40.

MCLEOD, J. (1993) *An Introduction to Counselling*. Buckingham: Open University Press.

MEARNS, D. AND THORNE, B. (1988) *Person-Centred Counselling in Action*. London: Sage.

MERRY, T. (1994) An analysis of ten demonstration interviews by Carl Rogers: implications for the training of client-centred counsellors. *Paper for the Third International Conference on Client-centred and Experiential Therapy*, Austria.

MERRY, T. AND LUSTY, B. (1993) *What is Person Centred Therapy?* Loughton, Essex: Gale Centre.

MILLER, A. (1983) *For Your Own Good*. New York: Farrar, Straus and Giroux.

MILLER, A. (1984) *Thou Shalt Not Be Aware*. New York: Farrar, Straus and Giroux.

MILLER, A. (1987) *The Drama of Being a Child*. London: Virago.

MILLER, A. (1990) *Banished Knowledge*. London: Virago.

MILLER, A. (1992) *Breaking Down the Wall of Silence*. London: Virago.

MONTESSORI, M. (1912) *The Montessori Method*. London: Heinemann.

MORRIS, C.W. (1956) *Varieties of Human Value*. Chicago: University of Chicago Press.

NATIELLO, P. (1987) The person-centred approach: from theory to practice. *Person Centred Review* 2, 203–16.

NATIELLO, P. (1990) The person-centred approach, collaborative power, and cultural transformation. *Person Centred Review* 5, 268–86.

NEIL, A.S. (1926) *Summerhill – A Radical Approach to Education*. London: V. Gollancz.

NEIL, A.S. (1937) *That Dreadful School*. London: Jenkins.

NYE, R. (1991) *Three Psychologies*, 4th edition. New York: Brooks/Cole.

PATTERSON, C.H. (1984) Empathy, warmth, and genuineness in psychotherapy: A review of reviews. *Psychotherapy* 21(4), 431–8.

PEDERSON, P. (1987) Ten frequent assumptions of cultural bias in counseling. *Journal of Multicultural Counseling and Development* 15, 16–22.

PERVIN, L.A. (1989) *Personality*. New York: Wiley.

PONTEROTTO, J. (1987) Counseling Mexican Americans: A multimodal approach. *Journal of Counseling and Development* 65, 308–12.

PONTEROTTO, J. AND BENESCH, K. (1988) An organisational framework for understanding the role of culture in counseling. *Journal of Counseling and Development* 66, 237–41.

PULKKINEN, L. (1982) Self-control and continuity from childhood to adolescence. In:. Baltes, P.B. and Brim, O.G.(Eds) *Life-span Development and Behaviour*, Vol. 4. New York: Academic Press.

RICHARDS, A.C. AND RICHARDS, F.L. (1988) Roundtable Discussion. *Person Centred Review* 3(1), 104–28.

RIDLEY, C.R., MENDOZA, D.W. AND KANITZ, B.E. (1994) Multicultural training: reexamination, operationalization, and integration. *Counselling Psychologist* 22(2), 227–89.

ROEBUCK, F., FLORA N., BUHLER, J. AND ASPY, D. (1976) Cited in Rogers, C.R. (1983) *Freedom to Learn for the Eighties*. Charles Merrill.

ROGERS, C.R. (1951) *Client-Centred Therapy: Its Current Practice, Implications and Theory*. Boston: Houghton Mifflin.

ROGERS, C.R. (1957a) The necessary and sufficient conditions of therapeutic personality change. *Journal of Consulting Psychology* 21(2), 95–103.

ROGERS, C.R. (1957b) A note on 'The Nature of Man'. *Journal of Counselling Psychology* 4(3), 199–203.

ROGERS, C.R. (1961) *On Becoming a Person*. London: Constable.

ROGERS, C.R. (1964) Toward a modern approach to values : the valuing process in the mature person. *Journal of Abnormal and Social Psychology* 68(2), 160–7.

ROGERS, C. R. (1970) *Encounter Groups*. Harmondsworth: Penguin.

ROGERS, C. R. (1973) *On Becoming Partners*. London: Constable.

ROGERS, C. R. (1978) *On Personal Power*. London: Constable.

ROGERS, C.R. (1980) *A Way of Being*. Boston: Houghton Mifflin.

ROGERS, C.R. (1981) Notes on Rollo May. *Perspectives* 2(1).

ROGERS, C.R. (1982) Reply to Rollo May's letter. *Journal of Humanistic Psychology* 22(4), 85–9.

ROGERS, C.R. (1983) *Freedom to Learn for the Eighties*. Columbus, OH: Charles Merrill.

ROGERS, C.R. (1986a) Reflection of feelings. *Person-Centred Review* 1(4), 125–40.

ROGERS, C.R. (1986b) Rogers, Kohut and Erickson: A personal perspective on some similarities and differences. *Person-Centred Review* 1(4), 375–7.

ROGERS, C.R. (1986c) The Rust Workshop. *Journal of Humanistic Psychology* 26(3), 23–45.

ROGERS, C.R. (1987) Comment on Schlien's article, 'A Countertheory of Transference'. *Person Centred Review* 2(2), 182–8.

ROGERS, C.R. (1989) The Case of Mrs Oak. In: Wedding, D. and Corsini, R. (Eds), *Case Studies in Psychotherapy*. Itasca, IL:F.E. Peacock.

ROGERS, C.R. AND DYMOND, R.F. (EDS) (1954) *Psychotherapy and Personality Change*. Chicago, IL: University of Chicago Press.

ROGERS, C. R. AND SANFORD, R. (1980). Client-centred psychotherapy. In: Kaplan, H., Sadock, B. and Freeman, A. (Eds) *Comprehensive Textbook of Psychiatry*, Vol. 3. Baltimore, MD: Williams and Wilkins.

ROGERS, C.R., GENDLIN, E.T., KIESLER, D.J. AND TRUAX, C.B. (EDS) (1967) *The Therapeutic Relationship and its Impact: A Study of Psychotherapy with Schizophrenics*. Madison, WI: University of Wisconsin Press.

ROWAN, J. (1975) Encounter group research: No joy? *Journal of Humanistic Psychology* 15(2).

SALEY, E. AND HOLDSTOCK, L. (1993) Encounter group experiences of black and white South Africans in exile. In: Brazier, D. (Ed.) *Beyond Carl Rogers*. London: Constable.

SANFORD, R. (1991a) The beginnings of a dialogue in South Africa. *The Person-Centred Approach and Cross-Cultural Communication* 1(1).

SANFORD, R. (1991b) Reflections on our South African experience. *The Person-Centred Approach and Cross-Cultural Communication* 1(1).

SMITH, M., GLASS, G. AND MILLER, T. (1980) *The Benefits of Psychotherapy*. Baltimore, MD: Johns Hopkins Press.

SMITH, P.B. (1975) Controlled studies of the outcome of sensitivity training. *Psychological Bulletin* 82, 29–48.

SMITH, P.B. (1980) *Group Processes and Personal Change*. New York: Harper & Row.

SUE, D.W. (1981) *Counselling the Culturally Different: Theory and Practice*. New York: Wiley.

THORNE, B. (1992) *Carl Rogers*. London: Sage.

TROSTLE, S.L. (1988) The effects of child-centred group play sessions on social-emotional growth of three-to-six-year-old bilingual Puerto Rican children. *Journal of Research in Childhood Education* 3(2), 93–106.

USHER, C. (1989) Recognizing cultural bias in counseling theory and practice: the case of Rogers. *Journal of Multicultural Counseling and Development* 17, 62–71.

VAN BELLE, H. (1980) *Basic Intent and Therapeutic Approach of Carl Rogers*. Toronto: Wedge Publishing.

VERHELST, P. (1991) Language and cross-cultural communication. *The Person-Centred Approach and Cross-Cultural Communication* 1(1), 61–68.

WAXER, P. (1989) Cantonese versus Canadian evaluation of directive and non-directive therapy. *Canadian Journal of Counselling* 23(3): 263–271.

WOOD, J.K. (1986) Mais principios de aprendizagem centrada na pessoa. Symposium paper – University of Sao Paulo, Brazil.

Index